The ABC's of Preschool

The ABC's of Preschool

Your Guide to Owning, Operating, and Thriving in Early Childhood Education

Ms. Amber Jayne

All Rights Reserved. No portion of this book may be reproduced, stored in a retrieval system, or transmitted in any form or by any means – electronic, mechanical, photocopy, recording, scanning, or other – except for brief quotations in critical reviews or articles without the prior permission of the author.

Published by Game Changer Publishing

Cover Design by Brian Halley/BookCreatives.com
Photo Credit: Jessica Feely
www.jessicafeely.com

Ms. Amber Jayne
Visit my website: TheLovingStartWay.com
Copyright©2023

Paperback ISBN: 978-1-962656-84-9
Hardcover ISBN: 978-1-962656-85-6
Digital ISBN: 978-1-962656-86-3

DEDICATION

To my amazing humans, Spencer, Wyatte, Colbey, and Gabriella, who were my inspiration in the creation and development of Loving Start.

I'm beyond proud of each of you for how you boldly take on life.
I'm grateful to have the beautiful title of mom for each of you.

You continue to bring great joy to my life every day.
Never forget to "Wish It, Dream It, Do It!"

I love you with everything within me.

To my team, who have stood by me and believed in me even in my darkest of days. Thank you from the very bottom of my heart.

Read This First

Just to say thanks for buying and reading my book, I would like to give you a couple of free resources!

Scan the QR Code Here:

The ABC's of Preschool

Your Guide to Owning, Operating, and Thriving in Early Childhood Education

Ms. Amber Jayne

www.GameChangerPublishing.com

Table of Contents

What Exactly Are the ABC's of Preschool?...... 1

Introduction – Wish It, Dream It, Do It 3

Chapter 1 – "A" Is for Adventure...... 9

Chapter 2 – "B" Is for Buildings 19

Chapter 3 – "C" Is for Community 29

Chapter 4 – "D" Is for Development 37

Chapter 5 – "E" Is for Employee...... 43

Chapter 6 – "F" Is for Franchise or Not 49

Chapter 7 – "G" Is for Goals 55

Chapter 8 – "H" is for Help...... 61

Chapter 9 – "I" is for Independence 67

Chapter 10 – "J" is for Juggling...... 71

Chapter 11 – "K" Is for Kindness and Love 75

Chapter 12 – "L" is for Laws 81

Chapter 13 – "M" is for Money 87

Chapter 14 – "N" is for No...... 91

Chapter 15 – "O" Is for Operations 95

Chapter 16 – "P" Is for Philosophy 101

Chapter 17 – "Q" Is for Quiet 105

Chapter 18 – "R" is for Research 111

Chapter 19 – "S" is for Schedules 115

Chapter 20 – "T" is for Training 121

Chapter 21 – "U" is for Understanding 125

Chapter 22 – "V" Is for Validation 129

Chapter 23 – "W" is for Wage 135

Chapter 24 – "X" is for X Marks the Spot 141

Chapter 25 – "Y" is for You've Got This 145

Chapter 26 – "Z" is for Zoom Away 149

What Exactly Are the ABC's of Preschool?

Welcome, my name is Amber, and I'm so glad you've found this book. I'm excited to share my "trade secrets" of running my own preschool for the past two decades. I've been in the early childhood education field since I was nineteen, teaching infants through transitional kindergarten, and I love this field. You could say it's in my blood.

In this book, I will teach you how to open, market, and run a successful preschool for the long term. This will not be a quick start-up or an easy journey. It will take dedication, passion, and determination to see your dream of being your own boss become reality.

This book will teach you how to gain respect and create a successful preschool with authority in your community. If you are passionate about little ones and early learning, this book will be your guide on how to run a thriving preschool that will be a consistent financial asset to your family.

I encourage you to journal and take notes as you read. I'll be sharing my successes, my failures, and everything in between that I've learned over the past twenty-five years.

The ABC's of Preschool will guide you to:
- **Create financial security through a rewarding career that is always in demand and where you can make a significant impact on your community.**

- **Spend more time with your children, with the flexibility to be there in their formative years.**
- **Be an early childhood education authority in your community by making a positive impact.**
- **Create, open, and operate your dream childcare center, one that will not only endure over the long haul but will also thrive for years to come.**

My wish is that as you read through this guidebook, I can help inspire you to pursue your passion for little ones and turn it into a thriving career where you are the boss. I want you to understand there is freedom and financial stability in owning your own school. Owning my own centers has been a beautiful and wonderfully unexpected blessing. It has helped shape my own children and has allowed me to make a difference in thousands of children's lives. Running my own preschool has gifted me financial stability and allowed me the freedom to be a full-time mom and traveler of the world, my other passion.

I am so thankful for my career, and I am thrilled to share with you my journey in this field so you can create your own successful career in it.

INTRODUCTION
Wish It, Dream It, Do It

"Dreams can come true, have the courage to pursue them."
—Walt Disney

So you want to start a preschool or daycare, right? My job here is to write a book on how to do that and keep you engaged the entire time. You may not even know how you came across this book or if you are qualified to open a preschool. You may be so far into parenthood or life and exhausted that the thought of doing something for yourself or starting a new business may seem too daunting. You may just decide to continue to binge-watch Netflix rather than dream up a whole new career.

But let's stop right here for a second. If you have found this book, I believe you are a dreamer; you have a passion to serve others. Maybe you already work outside the home. You're rocking "the mom life" and juggling the career, too. Kudos to you; I know it's not easy. Maybe you feel stuck working a job that doesn't feed your soul. You wake up every day, and it's the same thing day after day, and your current job isn't bringing you joy.

Whatever the reason, you are here right now reading these words, and I want to say thank you. I want to acknowledge the journey you are on. Every dream must start with a simple idea, then faith to believe we are capable of achieving it. But let's also be real, friend. The road to fulfilling our dreams is normally not an easy one. Many times, we can talk ourselves out of even starting because we don't believe we are capable. I have been in the early childhood field since I was nineteen, and I may be aging myself here because it's been over twenty-six years, but even with all my experience, I can also hear the voice of doubt in the back of my mind saying, *Who do you think you are?* Yet, I choose to ignore the little voice that sometimes plagues us all. That little voice is a normal part of most people's lives, but greatness comes to those who ignore it and move forward past doubt—to those who say, "I've got this."

I never imagined myself as an entrepreneur, or the owner of multiple preschools, or the CEO of my company. Those things were never on my radar. In fact, I never believed in big things for myself. I had dreams and goals, but I just wanted to be a mom, a teacher, and an author. Mom was my first wish, my biggest desire. Being a businesswoman never even came into my mind—that I was capable. But I was. I am. I learned, I failed, and I grew, and as the years passed, I grew better and better. I was capable, and so are you, if you want it.

You may be seeking more, dreaming of becoming more, searching for something bigger, and maybe you want to contribute financially to the family budget.

If you're reading my words, then I believe you and I have something in common. Although we love being parents and although we see it as the ultimate job, it is the hardest and most exhausting but rewarding role ever. I get it. I've been there. "Mom life" is hard. Parenthood is rough. It's challenging, and it's easy to lose yourself in diapers, sports, and extracurricular activities. Life, in general, is tough. Whether you have one child or multiple, your world no longer revolves around you but another human being.

I believe you can be both a mom and a business owner. Even though I often tell people that I didn't see this coming and that my career was unplanned, it's been one of my greatest accomplishments, besides raising four wonderful humans who are now on their own life journeys. It's allowed me to have the freedom to be an engaged and active mom and bring financial stability to our home.

Over the years, I've been asked to write down what I've learned and to share my expertise in early childhood education, specifically how to open a preschool. Now that my kids are grown, I'm deeply excited to share my knowledge and help others achieve their dreams. So, I guess this is the part where I'm supposed to talk about my qualifications and why I am an expert.

I simply see myself as a girl who had a dream, didn't give up, and went after it even when it was hard, though I had no idea what I was doing. What I did have was drive, determination, and a passion for little ones. If you have these qualities, then you, too, can do the hard work, and hopefully, with this guidebook, I can help you dive in faster and smoother than I did—giving you tools that took me many years to learn.

I've been in the early childhood field since I was nineteen, and I am forty-five as I write this book. I've spent over two decades on the carpet of many classes, talking, teaching, and loving on kids. I've changed countless diapers of not just my own four kids but hundreds of children. Vomit? Yep, I've been thrown up on a few times, too—recently, in fact. While holding a garbage can for one of my little ones, who was vomiting over and over, I was sprayed in the face and on my jeans. Yet I didn't react; I just calmly continued to hold the can and stroke her hair, telling her it was okay. That's preschool life. Then, wouldn't you have guessed it, I started vomiting two days later.

Preschool life is messy. It's not a glamorous career by any means. Most days, I'm dressed in jeans and a cheap shirt. Never wear expensive clothes while teaching preschoolers! By the end of the day, I'm usually a mess. My jeans have at least a little paint, dirt, or boogers on them, and my shirt is a little sticky from me sweating most days from the non-stop moving and chasing little humans all day. I wash my hands twenty-plus times throughout the day. But if you track your steps, know that in this field, you'll get a lot of them in during the day. Your workout is your job. From preschoolers climbing on the tables or trying to get into the sensory table and kids running with sticks in their hands, chasing their friends as you chase them, hoping they don't stab their friends, to wiping away tears from lots of falls and crashes, the wrong food in their lunch, or the bike not being free at just the right moment—this job is aerobics. The best part of preschool life? There is never the same thing twice. It's just impossible. Every day is different; they keep you on your toes day in and day out.

This may not be a glamorous job, but it is one of the most rewarding jobs ever! I may be biased since this is all I've ever done, but it truly has been a job that feeds the soul and can really impact lives.

Over the last twenty-plus years, I have worked within the walls of my schools. I'm not sure I would call myself an expert on anything because I'm still learning and far from perfect. I've messed up multiple times, and I've had parents angry with me and teachers upset. I'm constantly trying to juggle my personal life and business life, but mostly, I'm always changing. My schools change just as our children evolve and grow. I think that is what has kept me in this business for so long. Embracing change, acknowledging when things aren't right or need a good kick in the pants, learning new techniques or new ways to look at early childhood education.

If you're reading this, you may be considering opening your own school or maybe want to learn more about this amazing career. It's not an easy choice or path, that's for sure, and there is a learning curve, but the rewards last, and touching little human lives is a privilege.

When you are dealing with kids, extra care must be taken. Parents are protective of their children, and rightly so, which makes preschool life a delicate job. You need so much love in your heart, with a generous dose of patience.

Children are our future, so this job must be taken seriously each day. If you have a hint of annoyance for little ones, then put this book down immediately. This is not the job for you, and that's okay. Everyone has their own passions and dreams. I have always said it takes a special person to teach preschoolers, and it is even more special to own and run a business that revolves around the care and education of children. But if you're like me and absolutely adore children zero to five, if you find amazement in the incredible growth of this age, and you want a career where you make a positive impact every day, then, my friend, I invite you to come along with me, and let's talk preschool: the good, the bad and the ugly.

It truly has been a game changer, both in the impact I've made in multiple communities and the financial freedom it's brought over the years.

CHAPTER ONE

"A" Is for Adventure

"The purpose of life, after all, is to live it, to taste experience to the utmost, to reach out eagerly and without fear for newer and richer experience."
—Eleanor Roosevelt

Some may not think of the childcare industry as an adventurous career, but I would have to disagree. Looking back at the past twenty-five years in this field, I would say it has been quite the adventure—one I would never have seen coming. It was an adventure I stumbled into and then absolutely fell in love with and never thought of as a job. I loved my work, I loved teaching, I loved directing, and I grew to absolutely thrive as a CEO.

I never got a college degree, and to be honest, I only have the basic education needed for this field. I was a mom, first and foremost. This was something I stumbled into because, after four months of staying home with my firstborn, I realized I needed more and wanted something to conquer.

It was just a thought, a tiny seed of an idea, but in reality, this is how dreams start: with an idea that, if we choose, can be planted and, with time and care, can bloom into something more beautiful than we could have ever imagined.

I was twenty-two, and I had been married since I was nineteen. I had been going to college part time and was a new mother. The mother part was what I always wanted for my life. I *loved* kids. At ten years old, I was the neighborhood babysitter. I started earning money young and loved having my own funds. At fifteen, I worked at the after-school program at my school for $4.75 an hour. It's funny how we remember those little details. Every day, Monday through Friday, I would walk over to the preschool area where my mom worked, which was attached to my high school, and I would put on my maroon smock and fill its oversized pockets with gloves and Band-Aids.

Then, I would head out to the playground with a smile. I loved it. I loved seeing the kids, playing with them, hugging them, and passing out Band-Aids whether they were necessary or not. Kids love Band-Aids. I loved my job, I loved my smock, and I loved that for a few hours a day, kids would look up to me as if I were a teacher. At that time in my life, when people asked me the dreaded question most adults ask teenagers—"What do you want to do when you grow up?"—I would answer that I wanted to be a teacher. I also aspired to be an author, but being a teacher was higher on that list.

I left the after-school job two years later and got a job at a clothing store at my local mall. As a teenage girl, getting 50 percent off my clothes sounded pretty amazing. So, at seventeen, I got my second real job. I worked nights and weekends, and my pile of clothes on my bedroom floor grew larger by the week. Looking back, I believe this simple job as a clothing associate really began to shape me into a CEO, although, at that time, I had no idea. During my time at the clothing store, I went from associate to assistant manager to manager. The store ended up going out of business, so a liquidator team was brought in. The main managers bailed, and I was the only one left standing. I was put into the manager position for the next six months as they closed down the store.

I learned how to hire, do the weekly schedule, and do all the money deposits at the end of the night. I loved it, too. I loved being in a leadership role and taking ownership of the store even though it was about to close. That job taught me so much. I didn't realize those life skills laid a foundation for my own business years later.

Life is an adventure, whether we want to see it or not. None of us probably saw how our lives have ended up. Maybe we had some sort of road map or plans to start with—we all had dreams of becoming something or someone when we were young, but then we ran into our adult lives at full force, only to be slammed into a wall once or twice or maybe quite a few times and shaken into the reality that adulthood is not easy.

I often say if we could see our future, maybe we wouldn't even get out of bed. Life is a beautiful yet messy gift and one hell of an adventure.

No matter where you are in life now or how you got there, we only have right now. What do you want to do right now? Are you ready for a new adventure? If you're reading this, then you must love kids, or you may have dreamed or thought about opening your own preschool.

You may be wondering if you can do it, if you're up for this adventure. I say yes. If you really want it and are passionate about kids, then yes — you can do it.

When I had my first son at twenty-two, my plan was to stay at home. My own mother was a stay-at-home mom for most of our childhood. When we got older, she worked part time. In my head, I always imagined myself staying home with my kids. When they got older, I would teach kindergarten. That was the plan. That was part of my road map to my dream life as an adult.

But when my son was four months old, I quickly realized I was lonely at home. Before I go any further, let me acknowledge something: there are two sides when you become a mother, and I really felt this as a new mother—you are part of the working mothers club or the stay-at-home mothers club.

Today, my oldest is twenty-three, so maybe this has changed (I'm hoping this has changed). But when I was twenty-two and a first-time mother, I felt the divide acutely. I wanted to stay home, and I wanted to be proud of being a stay-at-home mom, but I quickly realized that folding the laundry every day and cleaning the kitchen over and over made me feel resentful. (Oh, ouch. . . that's honest.) No one clapped or cheered when another basket of clean clothes was put into the dresser. No one praised me for unloading the dishwasher for the third time that day. Of course, my husband at the time told me I was great and a wonderful mother. But that seemed to not count in my eyes. I'm not sure why. I was raised by a mom who stayed at home, so it was familiar to me. It was what I thought I wanted. As I share my own feelings, I don't judge anyone who stays at home with their kids. Honestly, that is awesome, and it's a gift for sure.

For me, I felt as though I was losing myself in motherhood, and only four months in, I knew I needed to go to work, even if it was part time. I loved, loved my son. He was the best baby, but I wasn't the best version of a mom for him yet. I was lonely, and the house felt like a cage. I decided to apply for a job at a local high-end gym near my house to work in the childcare center so I could bring my son. I got the job. Not only could I take my son with me to work, but I got a free membership to the nicest gym around. I felt as though I had purpose again besides being a mom.

I liked my job and began meeting other moms there. So many of us had babies the same age. It was awesome, and I found a wonderful community of ladies. The perks were when I did use the gym, I knew all the ladies who were working, and they took such good care of my son, even if I skipped my workout just to sit in the lounge with a book and my feet up for an hour.

I was now working part time, and I loved it. I still kept a clean house, I still did the laundry and the cooking, but I also got a paycheck. Though it was small, I felt as though I was contributing, and the house didn't feel like a cage anymore.

It wasn't long after I started at the gym that I realized kids and preschool-age kids were my passion. When I graduated high school, I went to junior college and got my early childhood education units. My first job was at nineteen as a two-year-old teacher. I loved it. A lot of people didn't want to teach the twos, but I was young, and since this was my first job, I didn't know any better. Yet I fell in love with the age and teaching. I enjoyed reading books and singing and holding them tight when they were sad or upset.

I worked at my first preschool for a year and ended up getting fired from that job. Yep, I was fired. My co-teacher was amazing and was such a good person and a teacher. The management at this school kept promising her a management position, but she was there for four years, and they would repeatedly promise her things and never come through. One day, I had had enough. I marched into the director's office and asked about this, and told them they had an amazing employee they wouldn't want to lose. That conversation didn't go over well. I was told it was none of my business. So that night, I wrote a letter, printed it up, and passed it out to all the staff at the school. I don't remember exactly what the letter said; it was probably that the director kept promising things but didn't follow through, etc. Well, shortly after everyone got the letter, I was called into the office, fired, and escorted off the campus.

I had never been fired before, but I left with a smile.

At my next school, I taught junior kindergarten and again fell in love with that age group. More and more, I just loved to teach. But more and more, I was seeing the politics of preschools. I was learning how things were being run, how staff were treated, what I liked, and what I absolutely hated. While at my second school, I became pregnant for the first time, and I also started to bleed in the middle of the day and miscarried my first pregnancy. I quit shortly after my miscarriage. I needed a fresh start.

My third school was my favorite. There I learned so much about good management and how a preschool program could not only be full time but also successful part time.

I was in charge of forty students. Yes, forty! The school was part time, and I was the main teacher Monday through Friday, so I had five different classes and forty students to keep track of as well as families. I took ownership quickly. I was expected to change out my bulletin boards weekly, keep a super-organized, clean class, attend staff meetings, and keep track of and turn in all of my curriculum. This was where teaching got real, and I was a teacher—a real teacher. At this school, I got pregnant again. I was so thrilled but also terrified. I worked at the school for only a year because my due date was in December, and I ended up leaving before the new school year. But that job was pivotal for what was to come next.

Still, I had no plans of opening and operating my own preschool. I was just living life, dealing with the adventures life threw at me, learning how to navigate my grief through my miscarriage and then the joy from giving birth to my firstborn, extremely healthy son.

Life is an adventure, and it's up to us how we deal with it.

All my previous jobs—the neighborhood babysitter, the after-school provider, the clothing store manager, being fired for standing up for my co-worker, the part-time school, and head teacher of forty students—were laying the foundation for who I was becoming and how I would run my future school. Even though I had no idea then, looking back, I realize I use all of those skills now on a daily basis.

I am a firm believer that life experience is the ultimate teacher. You may not have a college degree, you may have one but not in a field you are passionate about, or you may be a first-time mother or a grandmother longing for fulfillment. This career in early childhood education and starting your own daycare/preschool could provide a missing link.

Sometimes, the road we think we have mapped out really isn't the right road at all, and by accident, we find a different road. Or maybe it is not by accident at all. Maybe we had to go on the first road first to get to our next adventure.

At twenty-two years old, I loved being a mom. It was what I always wanted, and that didn't change. But what was changing was that I needed more to challenge me, to awaken me.

While working at the gym, I started to dream. I started to get a crazy idea: *What if I opened up my own preschool?* Mind you, I had no college degree, I hadn't taken any business classes or had any experience running my own business. I didn't even know what an entrepreneur was. But something inside me started to dream. I would take notes, run numbers, and create a schedule of classes. I presented it to my husband at the time. I showed him my ideas and how much money I thought I could make. I started to research licensing, which I'll get into more later in the book. People opened their own home daycares all the time. But I didn't want to be like all the others. I didn't want to be identified as a daycare. I wanted to be a preschool with curricula and with a focus on teaching.

Here is where Loving Start (formerly Smart Start) Preschool was born (now Loving Start Learning Centers)—at my kitchen table with paper and lots of notes and numbers. I wanted both worlds; I wanted to work and stay at home with my son and future kids. I wanted to be an awesome mom but also teach.

So the tiny seed of an idea was planted, and over the next six months, that little seed was watered—a lot.

Two weeks after 9/11, when our world was shaken to its core, I opened in October with four kids. My dream was becoming a reality, and within six months, I had forty-eight students and a waiting list, all running out of my house.

Loving Start Learning Center (formerly Smart Start) opened in October 2001, and the adventure was only just beginning. I took a chance on my dream and myself, and what a wild, fulfilling, and, at times, crazy-stressful adventure it's been. But if I had to do it over, I would do it again and again.

Are You Ready for the Adventure?

In this guidebook, I want you to plant your own seed, your own ideas of how your very own preschool will look, feel, and be run. Use this book as a tool to create and take notes in every chapter. Sometimes, to truly make a dream a reality, you must first begin to write it down—see, read, and believe it. So get messy, scribble, and journal; this is your guidebook to your future as a preschool owner. I was just a mom with no college degree and no experience except a few years of teaching. But what I had was a deep passion for little ones. If you have that passion, let's begin our journey to possibly one of your biggest adventures yet.

In this guidebook, I will cover "The ABC's of Preschool" and so much more. We will talk about choosing a building, developing your program, money, staffing, and philosophy. By the end, I feel confident that with your notes, you will be set up for success as you begin to launch your own preschool.

I've learned a lot over the past twenty-plus years, but I've also experienced many failures. I'm excited to share both my successes and failures, so that one day, you can embark on your very own preschool ownership adventure.

Journal Prompt

Why do you want to read this book?

_____
_____
_____
_____
_____
_____
_____
_____
_____
_____
_____
_____
_____
_____
_____

CHAPTER TWO

"B" Is for Buildings

"Whatever good things we build end up building us."
—Jim Rohn

Over the years, I have opened up multiple schools in multiple-sized buildings. But for the first nine years of Loving Start history, I ran my preschool from my home. Buildings cost a lot but can also serve more clients. I often recommend that newbies to this business not just jump right in with a giant lease but start small. Make sure you love the work, make sure you are profitable first, and then, in time, maybe take the leap from home to commercial. The truth is, the leap is pretty big, and so is your overhead.

Finding the right building is oftentimes the hardest challenge in this industry. Childcare centers are very specific and have to meet certain state and city guidelines. This can make finding the right building somewhat of a challenge. But don't get discouraged.

In October 2001, I opened up Smart Start (now Loving Start) in my living room. Now, this was just the first phase of my vision. Six months prior, I completed all of the qualifications required for the state of California to open up a home daycare. I had my home inspected, went through CPR/first aid training, filled out applications, and finally had my home visit. I just needed my license in hand so I could start advertising. My vision was to create a preschool that was separate from my home. I wanted home life and work to be separate. My dream was to have a classroom built onto the house with its own entrance. In order to do this, we had to take a big risk that felt incredibly scary. We didn't have a lot of money, so this was a huge leap of faith in my little seed of an idea.

My then-husband and I took out $30k from our home and, with his carpentry background, started to build an addition to our house. In the meantime, I bought tables and chairs and turned our living room into a classroom. I created curricula and didn't use the word daycare in any of my marketing. I was going to set myself apart from all the other home daycares in the area. I wasn't going to market it as a daycare; I was going to be a real preschool, one that just so happened to be located in a residential neighborhood in my home. I was creating a school where I wanted my kids to go—where they would feel loved, have the chance to be messy, and begin to grow a true love of learning. When Loving Start opened, I was also pregnant with my second child. So, as I created Loving Start, I did it with my kids in mind and how I would want them to learn and be taught.

Construction started on the addition, and our living room was transformed into a classroom while the classroom was being built. Family photos were removed from the walls, and in their place were bulletin boards. Instead of our used couch, little plastic chairs and tables were set up. It was adorable, and I loved my living room classroom. But it would only be temporary. The goal was to keep family life and business separate.

As I mentioned earlier, I opened weeks after 9/11. It was a scary time for the country, and it felt even scarier opening up a new business during such a stressful period. I was asking parents to leave their children with me part time after everything that had just happened.

I opened an afternoon class first, a small preschool class with four students, as I continued to work at the gym. Two of the students were paying, and two were free. I needed kids to have a class. Three of the kids were from the gym—I would bring them home with me from work—and the other one was my nephew. But it was a start, and I loved those four students. I was professional, and my title was Ms. Amber. I created my weekly curriculum, art projects, songs, books, letters of the week, and a number of the week. I was organized and intentional, creating a little outside-the-box preschool program. I'll cover teaching philosophy later, but I didn't want to fit into a box of any kind.

There are different philosophies and teaching styles in the world of early childhood education, mainly created by people who are long gone now. I didn't want to subscribe to any one of them. So I didn't—I embraced them all.

In April of 2002, my classroom was ready, and my little school wasn't so little anymore. I had people lining up to sign up for my program. My classroom was off my living room, with a door that kept the two rooms separate. My families would enter the side yard and come in through the white door to my world—my little school room. It had a bathroom, a counter, and a sink with lots of windows. By the time the classroom was opened, I was full. I had forty-eight students in a matter of six months. I also brought in two other teachers to help, as I was running two classes five days a week. The last preschool I had worked at, the one I loved, where I had forty students, really prepared me for this moment. All the knowledge I gained there came into play as I began Loving Start. My building was small, but it was attached to my home, so my home became a write off. For tax purposes, it was awesome, and it also created a fun space for my kids to play.

For nine years, I ran my business this way. We moved twice along the way, and both times, we intentionally looked for a home that had a family room with its own door to the outside and a way to separate it from our home. For those nine years, I operated with four different classes during the week, and my yearly calendar took all the same holidays as the local schools.

Our third move in 2006 was the biggest. We were moving two hours away, leaving all our family and friends to live in the country in the small town of Loomis, California. A few months before, I had no idea there was even a town called Loomis.

By then, I was a mom to three young boys, and they were my world. I had created my school so I could do both—work and be a mom. All of my boys were also students at Loving Start. We were also expecting our fourth, our daughter, who we were in the process of adopting. But we wanted a small town and land and farm animals for our kids, so we took a huge leap and bought a home with almost three acres. The house worked well for a school, and since the business was going so well in the Bay Area, we decided to keep the house there, put in renters, and keep that school open.

Now a mom of three and waiting patiently for our fourth, I wasn't just running one preschool out of my house, but I was about to open another school in a 6,300-person town where I knew no one! I quickly went through the licensing process as fast as I could and prepped our new home for the state visit, and as soon as I got that license, I dove into marketing.

I bought all new furniture and made what was once a family room into another adorable classroom. This time, our school backyard was giant, and we got goats and chickens. The appeal of this quiet little town was the ability to provide a preschool "farm school."

We moved at the end of August, and by October 2006, I opened up Loving Start Loomis. It was kind of funny that it was again in October when I found myself opening my second school five years later.

I hired my first teacher right away, as I needed help so I could teach and be a mom, and it wasn't long until Loving Start was full. Our daughter came home in November 2006, so I was again a new mom starting a new school. I wasn't only juggling being a mom of four, but I had two schools to manage, and one was two hours away. Two homes with two preschools attached. To be honest, it wasn't easy. I was also contracted to consult a friend on her new school in the town over from mine in the Bay Area. So, in reality, I was juggling three schools.

This business allowed me to help provide for my family, be a mom, and attend soccer practices, baseball practices, games, and whatever else was going on. I only worked in the mornings and had staff for the afternoons, though when my kids were nursing, I wouldn't work as much, and I had a nanny part time when I taught. Sometimes, I taught Monday, Wednesday, and Friday mornings and had Tuesdays and Thursdays off. Other times, I only worked Tuesdays and Thursdays. I loved my work more than any other job. I loved serving my community, and I loved providing jobs.

Eventually, having two schools and four little kids became a lot. So, it was time to sell our home in the Bay Area and also sell my first Loving Start. I approached one of my current clients who also wanted to work at the school. It all worked out, and in 2008, they bought our home and the school. It was my first time selling a school, and little did I know it wouldn't be my last.

In November 2009, I got a phone call toward the end of my breast cancer journey at thirty-one. Yep, I am a proud cancer survivor, and I'll share more about my life-changing cancer diagnosis later in the book. As I was preparing for another surgery, an amazing opportunity fell into my lap. When opportunities arise, my usual answer is "Yes," and then I try to figure out the rest later.

One day, I got a call from someone telling me there was a preschool around the corner from our old house that we had sold a year before that was up for lease. It was a 2,400-square-foot school with three classes in a commercial building, and they asked if I was interested in it. Without hesitation, I said, "Yes." This was two hours away, right around the corner from where I'd sold my first Loving Start in the house. The new owners had changed the name, so I knew I could open back up, but this time in a commercial building.

So, two days after my breast implant surgery, I was filling out my first center license application eight years after I opened Loving Start in my living room. With my new breasts came a new school and a new building.

In February 2010, I opened my first commercial building preschool center. A cute yellow school in Newark, California, right back where I was only a couple of years before. This time, I leased the building and was running a medium-sized center. I hired a full staff: six teachers and a director. I had an open house, and my license wasn't just for twelve students like my home preschools. I was licensed for forty-eight students at one time. We even had a ribbon cutting.

I had survived cancer and, in that same year, grew my business exponentially.

Right before I was diagnosed with breast cancer in March of 2009, we had started construction on a remodel of an old barn on our property in Loomis, California. We were working our way through the city's red tape, permits, licenses, construction, and lots and lots of inspections. The building was on our property, but the city had approved us to open up a commercial building, granting us a use permit. In May 2010, Loving Start Loomis's new building was finished, and we had another ribbon cutting and huge celebration.

In the same year, I opened up two centers. I never saw that coming. The Loomis school would be licensed for thirty. I now called myself mom turned CEO.

Then, I got really ambitious and started seeking out buildings to expand in the area I lived in. If I could do two centers, why not three? It was all about finding the right building.

If you want a commercial building, it may take some time. Let me be honest; it may take a lot of time. There are lots of commercial buildings for medical or office use, but you need to make sure the building can get a use permit for childcare. With the building space, you are also looking for outdoor playground space. This is why you can't rush the commercial building search. It takes time and sometimes asking the right people to aid in the search.

Do you want to start in your home? Here is what you may need to set yourself apart:

Home-Based Building

1. Do you have a room with its own entrance and bathroom? (This creates a separate space, a self-contained classroom. It's not

necessary, but it allows you to enjoy your home for personal use, and it doesn't bleed into your peace.)
2. Is there a yard so the kids can safely play outside?

As you can see, the home building is pretty simple and can be up and running quite quickly after you pass your state inspections and application process.

Commercial Building
1. *Classrooms.* You are allowed students based on the square footage of the rooms. In California, it's 35 sq. ft. of space per child.
2. *Office.* This is important for your copy machine, where you will hold tours, etc., and is where sick kids can go.
3. *Bathrooms.* In California, you must have one toilet and sink per fifteen kids. Again, each state is different. Plus, you need a staff bathroom that is separate from the students'.
4. *Infant Center?* If you choose to offer care for infants, they will need their own space and a space big enough for a separate nap area for cribs.
5. *Yard.* Don't forget an outside space. In California, you need 75 sq. ft. per child in the playground.

These are the big things, making it tricky sometimes to find the right building. If it was a school before, then snatch it up quickly; it's always the easiest to get it licensed again or approved to open as a school. The hardest is if it hasn't been a school; then it can be quite complicated with the fire marshal and your state and city regulations. It's a gamble on whether it will be approved or not.

I found a large commercial building that was once a large franchise school. It was over 8,000 sq. ft.—big and empty. In January 2011, I leased that building, and I don't think I would ever do that again, but I learned a lot...

about what I *didn't* want. But I was on a roll, and if cancer couldn't get me, I was about to take more risks.

The lease was so expensive—it was a challenge. I painted the building inside and out and put my name on it. I hired staff, and students started to come. Going from your home to a medium-sized and then a *huge* center was quite the leap and a lot of financial risk and stress. There I was, trying to manage my stress differently since getting cancer, and I jumped into the biggest financial stress ever. My overhead was large. Even with a few months of free rent to get up and running, the cost of staff, rent, and utilities was well into $20k a month. It took many months to break even. I opened up my first infant center with that school. I was really a CEO now, managing over fifty employees and three different centers while not missing a beat with my kids, volunteering at their school, and being a team mom, all while hiding (very well, I might add) a very rocky and hard marriage.

The big center didn't bring me a lot of joy. When looking at a building, you have to really look at the lease and work backward. Can you afford the lease? And when looking at a huge space, think of the utility costs. Some months, it costs thousands of dollars to heat and cool it. The overhead was quite large.

I did get a lot of satisfaction from the blank canvas, transforming a building into something beautiful, and it brought joy to provide jobs. But financially, the bigger the center or building you have, the more money is going out, and a lot of pressure comes with it. It can be done, of course, successfully. For me, maybe it was the timing or maybe it just wasn't for me personally, but my happy spot is my medium school size.

There are options on the building, but if it's commercial you are seeking, you must make sure it can become a school. The best finds are the buildings that were previously a school or your home. Is it possible for you to add onto your home or move to a home that has the option of having a separate classroom? That can bring a good amount monthly, freeing you from large leases and overhead and, most importantly, the stress that comes with large commercial buildings. Whatever you choose, it's out there for you!

Journal Prompt

What kind of building do you see your dream preschool in?

CHAPTER THREE

"C" Is for Community

"Without community service, we would not have a strong quality of life. It's important to the person who serves as well as the recipient. It's the way in which we grow ourselves and develop."
— Dr. Dorothy Height

One of the biggest gifts that has come out of opening my school is the gift of community. Not only in how I've hopefully impacted the communities I've served but, more importantly, how much they have touched my life. Our community is like an extended family if we choose to see it that way. When you choose a career like early childhood education, it is a powerful tool to help other families in the community. Opening your doors is the first step. Providing excellent care is the next step. The third is when you can step in and go above and beyond to help a family with emergencies no one sees coming. But the most precious gift of all is when your clients, those amazing families in the community, rally behind you if you ever find yourself in a crisis like I did when I was going through cancer.

"Community" is a powerful word and a wonderful mission to help fuel your childcare. In fact, "community" is the word of the year for my center for the new year, focusing on our community and how we, as a school, can give back.

When I was twenty-three years old and starting my little preschool, I had my community in mind. I was a new mom, and I was in an amazing mother's group. In fact, all these years later, FUN Mother's Club is still going strong.

I had always longed to be a mother and was great with babies and kids. Yet, when I had my firstborn, I felt very lonely. It was then that I joined this club, or rather, this community. Of course, I didn't just join; I figured the best way to get to know people was to volunteer and become a board member. It changed the course of my early days as a mother. I didn't feel so alone. The best part wasn't just the different playgroups I could attend but the mom's nights out. Those nights were cherished. Gathering with a community of women solo, no husband and no child, I could see a little piece of just me again. Of course, we laughed, we drank, and we swapped stories of raising our babies and toddlers. We shared our struggles and shared advice when asked. That community was a gift, and now, even after twenty-two years, I am still in contact with many of the moms via social media. Now those babies are all grown up.

Community is a vital part of opening and running a successful childcare and preschool. And when you think of community, it is all-encompassing. Your community is where you will advertise, find your families and clients, and where your reputation will live. Your community is somewhat the heart of your business. It's where you will serve and give your love. If you really think about it, it's a big responsibility and should not be taken lightly.

How do you want to serve your community? How do you want people to talk about you or your business? Reputation is huge, and the way we serve people will either leave an everlasting mark of positivity or, heaven forbid, one of negativity.

Now, we can't please everyone; that is just a given. But if we open our hearts and arms with love for our students and families, we will be successful.

When I think of my community, I think of my customers and customer service. Think about the word "customer." I usually say to my teachers and directors that customer service is custom-sized, meaning each child and each parent is unique. All come with different expectations and needs to be met. There is no one-size-fits-all philosophy. Customer service is meeting every client where they are and going above and beyond not just as a whole for the entire community but individually, for the one in the bunch—customizing your service.

I was a young mom in a community of moms, and when I became a member of this mother's club, I had just begun Loving Start. Remember, I simply loved kids, I loved teaching, and I loved being a mom. I wanted it all: to teach and be a mom. When I joined the Mother's Club, I started to realize how valuable this community was. Not only was I sharing in lasting lifetime friendships and being supported as a mother, but I also was figuring out that this community was one I could serve with my talents.

I wasn't knowledgeable about anything related to business. I never thought about marketing, budgeting, or staffing. My mom had stayed home, and my dad had worked the same job for thirty years. I had an idea of opening up my own school, but I didn't have the business savvy *yet*. But that didn't stop me. I learned, and one of my biggest realizations was recognizing how important community is.

It was part of the foundation of my program. My character and my relationship with many other moms in the club was impactful. I didn't join to gain clients; I joined because I needed support and wanted to be a valued club member. So, I attended functions, helped with functions, and helped host functions. I jumped in completely, and many of those relationships helped me fill my school when I finally did open.

I began to advertise within the club, giving great deals. I was quite shy to talk about work or my new venture at functions because I never wanted to come across as salesy or pushy. So, for most of my two decades opening and running schools, I've never been over-the-top open about what I do. I just love people and love to be connected and involved. I am a people person. So, if it came up in conversation, it was always natural. I'm not a salesperson in the typical way. I believe sales is in relationships and, over time, a gradual trust.

But that first community in my mother's group was key for getting the word out about my school.

In fact, I opened up mine first, and then two other ladies followed, opening their own schools similar to mine. I'll talk about that later. It happens, and it's the nature of the beast—people will copy what you do. Take it as a compliment.

Years later, when I was going through breast cancer, my little community of Loomis, where I had been serving for three years, flipped the script. I wasn't just serving them anymore; they took me in and showered me and my family with so much love and support. It was overwhelming, and honestly, I have tears in my eyes as I write this. This occurred in 2009 when my four kids were little, and thankfully, most of them don't even remember that time. Being told you have cancer at any age is scary, but as a thirty-one-year-old mother with four little kids, and elbows deep in raising them, it was gut-wrenching and terrifying.

Once I got that diagnosis, I was forced to join yet another community or club—one I never wanted to join: the cancer club. My life went from ordinary mom life—sports, school, and work—to attending doctor's appointments and running non-stop. This was where the script flipped, and all the years of service and going above and beyond for my communities paid off, and I was the one being served with grace and utter love.

It's hard to accept that one minute you are living your life normally, and the next, you are told you have something inside you trying to kill you. You don't feel sick or look sick, at least in my case. Yet, with the appointments and decisions that needed to be made, time was taken away and given to cancer and the diagnosis.

Our community of friends and clients I served all stepped in, and I had ten weeks of meals delivered to our house. Imagine that: *ten* weeks of meals. I remember lying in bed after surgery for many days and just hearing our front door open and quiet footsteps walking across the family room to the kitchen, the fridge opening, and then the quiet footsteps heading back out the front door. So many meals were brought to us, and I had no idea whose footsteps they were. They just held our family up in prayer, love, and food. Our community also stepped up and helped taxi our kids where they needed to go. After my bilateral mastectomy, I was in bed for quite some time recovering, but I never had to worry about my kids being taken care of.

I had to step away from the school as well. I just needed time to go to the doctor and get better. Everyone was so gracious; it truly was an incredible time to see how amazing humanity truly is. So many times, with the news and the media, we see the ugly, the evil, and the horrible stories. Yet there is so much beauty in our communities, our friends, our families, and just simply the human spirit.

I am a believer of karma; a believer in what you put out is what you will receive, but let me clarify this. Life is beautifully messy; I say this all the time. Life is a series of the beautiful and then the messy. It's the natural cycle of life and maybe how we learn, understand, and grow as humans. But there is another level, one that is a reflection of our character. I believe if we operate our everyday life with integrity and love as the center, it will radiate to others. Love is the answer to all things, I think. In fact, that very statement is tattooed on my left forearm with a plumeria flower in honor of my mom, who passed away in March 2018.

If we serve our community with integrity, love, and sincerity, the clients will come; they will trust us to take excellent care of their little ones.

Community is those around you, where you live, where you socialize, your church, or the schools your kids go to. Community is also your home daycare or your childcare center. Community is formed in many ways. Use your community to serve. The greatest gift of all is to give of ourselves. If you are thinking about opening up a preschool, whether it's in your home or in a center environment, you must think about your community as part of your foundation.

1. How do you want to serve your community?
2. How do you want to fill a need in your community?

3. How do you want to be different in your community?
4. How do you want others to see you as you serve in your community?

Being a childcare provider is taking on a huge role in the community. Taking care of little humans is a gift but also a giant responsibility. We need to take it seriously. Our care, love, and support for those little ones will overflow into their homes and our community.

There are also times when you will be on the receiving end of the blessings and love of your own community. What goes around comes around. Use your community to help guide you in creating childcare that will meet its needs. Your community is like an extended part of the family.

Journal Prompt

Who is your community? How do you see your community as an ally in starting your business? How do you want to be viewed in your community?

_____

_____

_____

_____

_____

_____

_____

_____

_____

_____

_____

_____

_____

_____

CHAPTER FOUR

"D" Is for Development

"Play gives children a chance to practice what they are learning."
—Fred Rogers

Here is what I like to think of as the fun and exciting part of starting your own preschool: the development of your program and brand. Development can cover a wide range of areas in your program. This is where you get to be creative, and you get to be the artist crafting your very own masterpiece. How do you want to run your school? What learning style suits you best? I guess what I'm really asking is, what are you passionate about? The development of your preschool is a direct reflection of you.

This is a crucial piece to the puzzle, so I suggest taking your time and really thinking about the development of your program as the heart and soul of your business.

Later in the book, I'll cover more specific philosophies used in early childhood education. The most famous are, of course, Montessori and Waldport, just to name a couple. These styles are widely known in early childhood education, and each offers different teaching philosophies. We'll get into more specifics on that later.

So, the development piece is the core of your preschool. Are you a gardener, or do you love to bake? If yes, you may want to incorporate gardening or baking into your curriculum.

When I first started out, I realized I had to be different and had to present a unique offer. I started in my home and ran that way for over nine years, but from the beginning, I knew there were hundreds of home daycares. I didn't want to be just like everyone else. I wanted to develop a program with substance and curriculum. My background, as short as it was because I was so young, was working at actual preschools and daycares. I had four years of experience teaching children ages two to five years old. I knew early on how I wanted to teach and how I didn't want to teach. I had worked with a lot of co-teachers who should have never been there in the first place. They were grumpy and short with the littles. I also worked with amazing teachers who ran their classes with lots of love and excitement for what they were teaching. When Loving Start was being created, I knew I needed to develop a program that created a passion for learning at an early age. I wanted my students to immediately feel loved and cherished the moment they walked through the door. So whether I realized it or not at that time, I see it clearly now—love was at the center of my development. I think love has always been the center of everything I have done.

Each child is unique, just as all of us are. That should be accepted and celebrated. I think sometimes in big corporation schools, a curriculum is provided for the staff and is taught the same way across the board, down to the way the art project should be finished. I hated that; it just doesn't work for all kids. Being the mom of four kids, all wonderfully different, I have watched this in their own educational experiences. I've seen a couple of my kids sail through school with no problems and two others struggle, and as a mom, watching your kids struggle is heartbreaking.

Public schools, and many big, corporate preschools/daycares, offer a "one way or the highway" philosophy—box-type learning. If a child doesn't fit into the box or learn just the way the curriculum is offered, there must be something wrong with that child. I have never been a follow-the-crowd kind of girl. Maybe it's because I was raised in a traditional, in-the-box, religious family. When I was younger, there were clear rules and a belief that if I didn't obey them, I was bad. I was an extremely good girl, and when I say that, I mean it. I was scared to mess up, and I was terrified to fail. I prayed all day, asking for forgiveness because I believed I had to do good and be good to be loved. Religion, strict religion, can place false ideology on a child. My younger years were spent feeling the weight of my imperfections and striving to be perfect. Yet we all know none of us are perfect, and none of us will ever be. Religion is a box—and I lived in that box for a long time. When I got married at the age of nineteen, I even wore that white wedding dress as a virgin. When I became a mom, that began to change. At twenty-two, holding my firstborn son, I started to question the very essence of the foundation of my entire life. I wasn't sure how I could put this beautiful, innocent little baby boy into a box and expect him to live his life with so many rules. I loved my son just as he was.

That was the beginning of my rejection of the box in every aspect of my life. As a child, I was raised to wait for Prince Charming to come rescue me, assured I would fall madly in love. As a child, I believed my husband would be my protector and provider. I laugh at this now. No, my husband at the time was definitely not my protector; in fact, I'm not sure he ever truly loved me. But that's another book. I'm so thankful that I began to forge my own path, and little by little, I broke down the walls of expectations set by my upbringing and by myself.

One of the best parts of my journey of breaking down the walls is finding my independence and developing my own rules for my life.

As a woman and a mother, one of the things I am most proud of is creating Loving Start. I wanted to provide for my family and myself, and I didn't need a Prince Charming to save me. I needed my own thing, and I am so incredibly thankful for my younger self believing in herself and pushing forward to create a life that fulfilled her.

Those early choices allowed me to finally walk away from an emotionally abusive marriage seventeen years later. The choices of developing my own preschool, the curriculum, the branding, and the reputation allowed me to be financially stable, which afforded me the ability to completely walk away from a life that was making me sick, and into a life that I never imagined would bring me so much joy.

I think it's crucial, especially as a woman, to have our own income, to have our own bank accounts, and to be able to stand on our own two feet. We need to raise our daughters to know they are capable of greatness with or without a man, just as they are. I didn't need saving, nor did I want it.

This is why the development of your childcare or preschool is so critical. How you develop it will either give you the ability for sustainability for years to come or not. Last year, I celebrated my twenty-third anniversary of Loving Start. That girl, the twenty-three-year-old me with a small idea for a school, could never have imagined back then where this school, this program, would lead me.

Development

So let's talk about development and all the areas this can include.

The first step is to start spying on your competition. Google the schools closest to you. Go to their websites, find out what they offer and what their hours are, and just get a feel for your competition. Then, figure out how you can be different. If you are going to open up a home daycare preschool, do you want to be known as a daycare or an actual preschool program? One reason I called myself a preschool was because I didn't want to be known as just a babysitter. I didn't want my program to have kids play all day or watch movies. I desired actual structure, art projects, and circle time. I wanted them to learn letters and numbers. I wanted them to be messy at the end of the day. What set me apart in the early days of running out of my home was the fact that I was a school. I created a separate space for my classroom. I had bulletin boards, a monthly newsletter, a yearly calendar, and a written monthly curriculum. Yes, I was in a home, but when the parents walked through the doors, I presented them with professionalism and branded marketing materials. I'm not sure I even knew what branding was, but I was adamant about developing something different. Plus, to make money, I needed clients; I needed students.

I developed a curriculum that brought in all the best of early childhood educators—a little Montessori for math and language, a little Waldorf for nature and gardening. I loved to cook, so I incorporated weekly cooking. I developed a hands-on curriculum that I could individualize for each student. Every child is different, just as all of us are. I recognized and celebrated their differences. One student might have loved art and wanted to paint their entire class time. That was okay. I might have had another who just wanted to sit on the carpet putting puzzles together. It all sounded good to me. I introduced all the elements of learning, and they could pick and choose what they wanted. But the funny thing was, with time, most of the time, all of my students wanted to do all the projects offered. The goal was to create a lifetime love of learning from an early age. This was done with love, grace, and acceptance for every student.

Development is coming up with the name of your school, your brand, your philosophy or mission, and a daily schedule and curriculum. If you can create all of this, you are already setting yourself up for success.

Remember, this is the fun part! If this has been your dream for a long time, what are you waiting for? Guess what? Preschools and childcare are always needed, always. Go for it, and start developing your dream school! You've got this!

Development Checklist
1. Name
2. Philosophy or mission statement
3. Curriculum
4. Daily schedule
5. Website
6. Facebook page
7. Instagram

8. Phone number
9. Set up classroom
10. Set up playground

CHAPTER FIVE

"E" Is for Employee

"Alone, we can do so little: together, we can do so much."
—Helen Keller

Where do I begin with this chapter? There is a lot to say in the business world about employees. First off, let's be clear that I don't like the word "employees." I use it to describe my teams to others sometimes, but I usually say "my girls" or "my team." To me, "employees" sounds cold and doesn't describe the whole story of their value.

Quite possibly, finding the right employees or team is by far one of the hardest aspects of any business, especially in the early childhood education field.

A young child needs love, respect, and kindness from a caretaker. Not everyone who walks through your door looking for a job can provide that. I have never and will never operate with desperation to get a warm body into the classroom. I would rather work long hours and do whatever it takes to care for my students than put a mean and unloving person near them.

This is where finding the right team members and keeping them is vital. Some may look at education as the most crucial aspect of hiring someone, but to me that is secondary and not that important. Of course, they must meet the state requirements to work in a childcare center, but having a degree or fifty units in early childhood education does *not* make someone a great teacher.

Yes, that person may look amazing on paper, but truly, it's the core of the person, their soul, their morals, and their integrity. This has been my compass when interviewing people, and I've interviewed a lot of candidates over the years. Some have been gems and have been with me for years or until their life moved in a different direction. Others fizzled out quickly.

Your team is the very heartbeat of your school or childcare center. We all know the saying, "Happy wife, happy life," right? Well, my saying is, "Happy staff, happy everything." Yeah, I know it doesn't rhyme, but I have always put my staff first over my clients. I've spoken this aloud on my tours when showing potentials my schools. I explain it this way: "If my teachers aren't happy here, then it trickles down to our students and affects everything in the program." My schools have always followed the local school district schedule, which is not typical. Preschools and childcare centers typically run year-round with very little time off. In this field, the pay isn't the greatest. I recognize this. So in trying to retain staff as well as provide a good job they would want to invest their time in, paid time off was a perk.

When I say your team is the heartbeat of your business, I mean it. As employers, it is our job to provide employment that brings joy and value to their lives. My team, my staff, feel like an extended family. I have always tried to go above and beyond to make sure they feel appreciated. A few ways I've tried to really show appreciation are monthly gifts on the first workday of the month—just a little basket or bag of goodies celebrating the new month ahead—staff meetings that include the social element, work meetings with beer or wine to get to know each other better and create a family atmosphere, flexibility when emergencies or hard times happen, and giving grace when needed. Life happens to all of us, and just as we would want grace given to us, we need to give it to others. If a parent has passed, I've given a week of paid time off. If a team member's child has an emergency, I've always tried to let them leave. It's rare when I have not given time off.

In order to be flexible, you also must overstaff. When you run with the bare minimum, you put yourself in jeopardy of injuries of students or out of ratio when you fall under the state guidelines of how many teachers you need per student. It also creates a stressful environment for everyone. Over the past twenty years, there have been times when we were short-staffed, or I made mistakes in hiring, or I didn't give as much grace as I should have. We are all human, and all of us make mistakes.

Transitioning from my small in-home preschool to a center was a learning curve for me. There was a shift that began to happen when I had to start putting on a CEO hat.

There is a fine line between your staff becoming your besties and running a business. As women, especially, we are caretakers naturally, empaths, and strive to keep the peace. Many of us don't like confrontation. But as the boss, when running your program, there will be times when you must make difficult decisions for the sake of the whole picture. As much as I appreciate and care deeply for my team, I've also had to learn to separate the care from the purpose of running a long-term, successful business. This was not an easy transition between the two thoughts. I still treat my team like they are an extension of the family, the Loving Start family, but ultimately, I have had to learn to remove some of my deep emotions, separating work from personal. When you get too close to your staff, you sometimes can ignore the issues at hand, you can turn a blind eye, and it gets into a gray area. I feel this is the hardest part of any business you are running.

Keeping quality staff takes honesty, open communication, and mutual respect. As employers, it's our role to help foster their growth as well. But we also have our own lives and our own problems. One downfall as a boss over the years was that I mixed my personal life into my business. I have always been an open book, mainly because sad, hard things happen to all of us. Sharing my "hard" has also helped me heal. But when my marriage was falling apart, it got messy in all aspects of my life. My world was shattering into a thousand pieces around me, except my business. Loving Start was my rock, my job was my rock, and that part of my life remained unchanged. I could go to work and forget my pain and hug and love on my students. This is where my lady boss title may have been a little shaky. I started to rely too much on my staff, putting them into hard situations. They would listen to my unraveling life, but I couldn't give of myself because I was falling apart. I still ran a successful school and loved my job, deeply grateful for my school, yet I felt utterly broken. This is where I, as the boss, realized I was creating a messy work environment. I started to shift more to CEO. I had to set boundaries, and I realized I couldn't carry the weight of anyone else's life, nor should I expect anyone to carry my burdens. It's a balancing act transitioning from a small business to a larger business. There is a delicate balance of wanting to create a family-like work environment but keeping boundaries up so your vision is clear for the bigger picture of overall business success and happiness. When you get too close, with emotions and feelings all tangled up, you may ignore behavior that isn't serving the business or your other team members. You must learn to be the boss, and as much as I hated that title over the years, you do have to embrace it.

It's healthy to have boundaries for both the staff and management. Plus, looking back, I see now that many of my team members carried me as I limped along, going through a traumatic and toxic divorce. That wasn't their role; I own that, and I will always be sorry for that. Again, being human is a raw and sometimes difficult journey. Looking back, though, I am incredibly grateful for my team—they truly are a gift. Sharing in someone's life for sixteen, twelve, ten, or seven years is a gift—one that I don't take lightly.

A boss is not a dictator. If you run your business that way, it may come back and bite you. When I'm at my school, I will change a diaper if needed, clean up barf if needed, and scrub toilets if needed. We are all the heartbeat of the school, and in that sense, I expect everyone, including myself, to jump in wherever is needed. Many preschools will have titles of *head teacher* or *aide*. I have always called all my staff *teachers*. No head teacher. Sometimes, we do have teacher aids to describe their role as maybe not having enough units yet to be left alone with children. But overall, there is an equality I am proud of. All is equal in my eyes, and all should be treated with love and kindness.

One question you must ask yourself when you are looking for your team is, what are your non-negotiables? What will you never tolerate? Then, you must stick with your non-negotiables. My non-negotiables are hiring someone who is unloving to children or disrespectful to their peers. Early learners need teachers in their lives who love their jobs and who are passionate about early education. I believe wholeheartedly that if we don't show love and kindness to our children, they won't thrive to their fullest potential. Just recently, as I opened a new school, I let go of three people in the course of six weeks because they lacked love. Their words to the students were harsh and unkind.

As hard as it is to let go of people, just rip the Band-Aid off. It's not worth having a bad apple; it brings down the entire team. I would rather pick up the slack myself than have a team member who is unkind. What are your non-negotiables? What kind of culture do you want to create at your center? Finding the right team takes time and trial and error. Don't be afraid to fire quickly, with the goal of creating your dream team. What you don't want is a reputation of high turnover. In this industry, the turnover rate is high, so make it a priority to quickly build a strong team and then treat them well. You know the saying, "If the wife isn't happy, nobody's happy." Think of your staff in the same manner. If your staff isn't happy, then the students aren't happy. They can pick up stress from adults. It's vital to treat your dream team with love and kindness and reward them with gifts and bonuses for a job well done. If you don't have a staff, you don't have a school. Period.

Journal Prompt

What kind of work culture do you want to create? What are your non-negotiables?

_____

_____

_____

_____

_____

_____

_____

_____

_____

_____

_____

_____

_____

CHAPTER SIX

"F" Is for Franchise or Not

"The insurance of working with a big, already successful franchise just gives the chance to do other things on a more personal level."
—Jason Statham

To franchise or not, that is the question. When I decided to open my own school, I don't think I knew what the word "franchise" meant. I was young and definitely not business savvy. I had the idea of starting my own preschool and just went with it. I came up with the name, the curriculum, and the marketing design. The internet was still relatively new, so back then, there wasn't even Google to help research "how to open up a preschool." What I had was my experience and knowledge of the schools I had previously worked at. I understood what I liked about some of the schools and what I hated. So, when I came up with the crazy idea of opening my own school, I simply moved forward with my limited knowledge. It took a long time to learn how to become a business owner through a lot of trial and error—and when I say error, I mean a lot of failures.

In the early years of running my preschool, I was stressed a lot. I knew how to teach, but learning to become an owner versus an employee was a huge shift. I took pride in everything I did—from the way the classroom looked every day to the newsletters, the parent handbooks, and my small staff. Looking back, I realize I was stressed because I struggled with perfectionism.

I wanted everything perfect all the time, but as we all know, that is not possible. I was trying to get a new business off the ground solo.

If a parent had something negative to say, it gave me high anxiety and worry. If a day didn't go how I wanted it to, I stressed about how I could be better, do better. Not only was I trying to learn to be a business owner, but I was also now the mother of two boys who were seventeen months apart and pregnant with my third son. Just as I was learning how to be a mother, I was figuring out how to be a boss.

I did recognize I didn't want to be like the "big-box schools," as I call them—the giant schools with the big buildings. So when I finally learned and understood what a franchised school was, I honestly thought they were too corporate and not me at all. I didn't realize back then that not all franchised schools have a "big-box mentality." My only true knowledge of these schools was the teachers I would interview when they wanted to come work for me. They would complain that they didn't like that the curriculum would be printed and handed to them and that they had to do everything a certain way. It didn't feel like a family, but like a bunch of rules set by someone way up on a high hill in an office somewhere. I strived to be different; I valued relationships in my school. I believed that all my students and staff were part of my Loving Start family—once a student, always a family member. But I believe it can be done differently; I think you can be a franchise and still hold on to an amazing work culture.

Over the years, as the internet has grown and social media has taken off, it's been a beautiful gift to be able to still be in contact with the parents of some of my students. To watch them grow up from a distance is a gift—especially the students who gave me a chance back in 2001 when I was running my first class out of my living room.

For me, a franchise was never an option, mainly because I didn't know it could be. At that time in my life, I just wanted to provide for my family. So, when this idea hit me, I started to crunch the numbers. I had no idea about the real figures, budgeting, marketing, or how to hire teachers. But I was a creative, a go-getter, a dreamer, and an entrepreneur, even though I didn't even know what that word meant. My mom stayed at home for most of my childhood, and my dad worked at a chemical plant, so growing up, I was surrounded by people who worked nine to five. I didn't know of anyone who owned their own business. So when I came up with this idea, it took a minute to convince my then-husband.

If I remember right, those initial numbers I thought I could make definitely took much longer than I expected. But even though I didn't know what an entrepreneur was, it knew me, and that is who I am through and through. And, like any good entrepreneur, I took a risk. I had this dream, this tiny seed of any idea, and I leaped off the mountainside and started to flap my wings, not even considering failure or that I could crash and burn.

I wanted to be a mom for my boys, to be there and be active in their lives, but I also wanted to earn my own money. I wanted to feel like an equal contributor to my family. And let me pause here. Every situation is different, and everyone has their own goals and passions, and I honor what works for them. For me, this crazy idea was the answer to my desire to work and be a mom.

As I grew, I brought in my first staff, so as my family grew and the school grew, I had help. I could nurse my babies and put them down for naps, all while other teachers helped teach the preschoolers.

I was also becoming quite successful in my little preschool. I had a waiting list and was making money from my home. It filled my cup. It fulfilled me; the school was like one of my babies. I loved it dearly, and it took me years to develop it fully, with lots of failures. But it was mine.

After nine years, I had the opportunity to open my own center outside of my house. It felt right, and the opportunity fell into my lap. So, I grew again and learned how to run a larger center. But it fueled me—the problem-solving, the decision-making; I thrived on it. But it took years to really learn how to run a truly successful preschool on my own. Looking back, I wish I had a coach; I wish I reached out for help from an expert. I can see the value of an expert because, well, let's face it, time is money. I think having a team behind me could have also eliminated a lot of the anxiety and pressure I put on myself.

Franchise

Let's discuss whether to franchise or not. What is a franchise? We'll start there. Think of Subway, McDonald's, you know—all the chain restaurants. Those are franchises. You probably already know that, but the beautiful thing about a franchise is that all the secrets of the brand of the business, all the blood, sweat, and tears the owner put in along the way, are wrapped up with a pretty bow and handed to the franchisee, the person buying into it. This doesn't mean you won't have to work to get your own model off the ground, but you will have a support team.

Benefits of a Franchise

You don't have to spend years forming and creating your own brand. You essentially get a complex and well-developed business model with a support team. Your learning curve is cut down because it's all there; you just have to implement the brand already built. All the secrets of the trade are there; you simply follow the outline.

Take McDonald's, for example. You want to open a burger joint? Well, you have all that advertising, recipe refining, and business building to do. Or you can buy into what Americans already love and be a franchise owner of that established business, running your own McDonald's with the business plan, prices, reputation, recipe, etc. already set in place. It's like a cheat sheet, except you buy that cheat sheet. Buying a franchise gives you the peace of mind that the brand has been successful, and in return, if you follow the outline they give you, you will be well on your way to success, too.

Purchasing a franchise also gives you instant credibility, especially if that franchise has been in the business for a long time. You can instantly use their marketing, story, and background to sell to your future clients. It gives you standing right out of the gate rather than proving to your community for a few years with lots of trial and error that you are credible.

Buying into a franchise also gives you a support team. Typically, if it's a good franchise brand, you will have support with questions that come up, training videos, on-site support, and yearly seminars and training. You won't be on your own but will have a cheering squad rooting you on all the time. The negative about a franchise is it's a guide, a well-developed plan you must stay on course with, and there are set guidelines and expectations.

With a franchise, the support and cheering team comes with a price; it's called *royalties*. Every month, you give royalties to the franchise brand. That money is for marketing and to provide support. When you franchise, you are buying into their proven philosophy and their expertise.

Who should you pick for franchising? Just like I say when I tour families in my centers—go with your gut. If you do go down the franchise path, do your research. Understand the franchise or brand philosophy on learning. Does it align with yours? Can you see yourself supporting that philosophy for years to come? What does their support and cheering team look like? Have they been around long enough to be a proven brand? Then, go with your gut. You will know when you find the right franchise for you. You will feel it in your heart. Or, after reading this, you may realize you're a natural entrepreneur. If so, then go get 'em! Start creating your dream school and take the leap off the mountain.

Journal Prompt

What path is right for you? A franchise, an existing successful program, or to start your own from scratch?

_____

_____

_____

_____

_____

_____

_____

_____

_____

_____

_____

_____

_____

_____

CHAPTER SEVEN

"G" Is for Goals

"Setting goals is the first step in turning the invisible into the visible."
—Tony Robbins

Do you have goals? Have you ever really stopped to think about them? I remember early on, I wrote down my goals. When I think of my childhood, I am always stumped about where I got my goal-setting or my strong desire to write a to-do list and check it off. I still do this to this day. When I get into my office, I always have three tasks I want to get done for the day. I write them down and then love the feeling of putting a check next to the finished item. I will even go as far as adding an item to my to-do list if I forget to include it, even after I've just finished the list. It makes me feel accomplished; it's as simple as that.

I'm not sure where my drive to accomplish came from. Even at social dinners with friends, I'll ask, "Where do you see yourself in a year or five years?" Having a vision for your life gives a person purpose, and setting goals keeps you on track in the pursuit. Goals are so important, especially if you are going to run your own business. I have been in business for almost twenty-three years, and I still write goals for my staff, for myself, and for the school's future. I never want to get complacent or think I've made it. We never "make it." I mean, what does "making it" even look like?

Now, I'm not saying that we have to jump onto the crazy-fast hamster wheel of work, constantly setting goals without ever taking a moment to stop and smell the roses. I strongly believe that we have to have work/life balance to have happiness and joy in our lives. I think for many years, I truly believed I had to achieve those goals and accomplish them to be deserving of love. But that's not love; that's not finding joy in life; that's just having a load of stress on you all the time because you constantly feel like you're not living up to your own expectations.

So, this is a tricky chapter. Goals: can we find a balance in setting them or having dreams yet not working ourselves into the ground? I'll be the first to tell you that this career is not easy. Yes, there are lots of rewards—you get so much joy from your students, and working with early learners is different every day, so there is never a day that is the same—but it's a demanding job and takes a lot out of you day to day. That's why it's vital to set goals that are realistic and include self-care.

I often hear stories about people owning a daycare or running a home daycare, where they work twelve hours a day, Monday through Friday, without any breaks. It's taxing and draining, putting them at risk for a weakened immune system.

Setting goals is indeed a crucial aspect of any endeavor, including opening and running a preschool. Goals provide direction, purpose, and a sense of accomplishment. They help you stay organized, focused, and motivated.

Here are some suggested goals to consider for yourself and your preschool business:

- ***Provide exceptional early childhood education:*** Make it your goal to offer a high-quality
  - educational experience for young children. Strive to create a nurturing and stimulating environment that promotes holistic

development, fosters a love of learning, and prepares children for future academic success.

- **Cultivate a positive and inclusive environment:** Aim to create an inclusive and welcoming atmosphere where children, families, and staff members feel valued, respected, and supported. Foster a sense of belonging, celebrate diversity, and promote empathy and understanding among all members of the preschool community.

- **Ensure the well-being and safety of children:** Prioritize the health, safety, and well-being of the children entrusted to your care. Implement comprehensive safety protocols and maintain clean and secure facilities. Foster a culture of wellness and prioritize the physical, emotional, and mental health of every child. Safety is a top priority daily. These little humans need our utmost attention. Your eyes must always be on them, and you must create a safe space to play, grow, and develop a love of learning. From the classrooms to the playground, you must be watching for hazards and danger. Remember, little ones get into everything, and it is our job to see ahead to the possible dangers.

- **Establish strong partnerships with families:** Recognize the importance of collaboration between families and the preschool. Strive to build trusting relationships with parents and guardians, maintaining open lines of communication and actively involving them in their child's educational journey. Foster a partnership that supports children's growth and development. When you establish strong relationships, you form friendships, and there is great value in actually caring deeply about your clients. This job is serving your families and students and listening to your clients. They know their children the best, and we must work together for the betterment of the child.

- ***Strive for continuous improvement and professional development:*** Commit to ongoing learning and professional development for yourself and your staff. Stay updated with the latest research, best practices, and advancements in early childhood education. Encourage your team to pursue professional growth opportunities and provide them with the necessary resources and support.

- ***Remember that goals can be a combination of service-oriented and financial objectives.*** Your goals should align with your values, passions, and aspirations. By writing them down and revisiting them regularly, you can track your progress, make adjustments when needed, and stay motivated to achieve greatness in your preschool business. For me, personally, at the end of the year, I look over the semesters and see what worked and what didn't. I figure out our weaknesses and strive to be better the next year. Just as we are aging every year and changing, so should our business. Our school should never become stagnant; we should always strive for better. Our communities evolve, and based on your clients, year after year, there may be different needs.

These, of course, are just examples; this will be your business. I encourage you to take some time to write your own goals. Maybe they will be a mix of personal and business. There is power in writing down your goals!

Journal Prompt

What is your motivation for your goals?

_____

_____

_____

_____

Top 5 Short-Term Goals

1. _____
2. _____
3. _____
4. _____
5. _____

Top 5 Long-Term Goals

1. _____
2. _____
3. _____
4. _____
5. _____

CHAPTER EIGHT

"H" is for Help

"Ask for help, not because you are weak. But because you want to remain strong."
—Les Brown

I touched on this a little bit in the last chapter, but sometimes, when owning your own business, it can consume you. You go into it wanting to help provide for your family, and you want more freedom with your time, but before you know it, you're working non-stop. Something about business ownership that not a lot of people talk about is that it can consume you.

When you work for someone else, you typically can leave your work there, in the office. You, as the employee, get to enjoy your weekends and nights and not feel the weight of all that transpires behind the scenes. When you own your own business, it follows you everywhere. It took me years to learn how to balance this. I was also a mom, and motherhood is all day, every day, and the business felt like that as well for a long time. When you're first starting out, you typically do mostly everything to start earning money and get on your feet. You may teach, direct, enroll clients, and prepare the curriculum—you are a one-person show.

But in time, as you expand, you may need help. It's okay to ask for help; in fact, when I started to bring others on, my business grew and became more profitable. When we are in the weeds all the time, our focus becomes clouded and almost tunnel vision because we barely have time to look up.

Another area of help is how powerful this job truly can be in helping others. This is a service business, and a lot of your heart and soul will be poured out into it, your students, and your staff. Over the years, I have played different roles along the way in the area of helping. I have offered scholarships, discounts, and extended time off for staff, all in the name of helping others. There is so much joy in giving and being able to make an impact on lives. I have never taken my role and the impact I can make lightly. Sometimes, just listening is all you need to do to help a client or your staff. We are all just trying to figure out this thing called life.

There is balance, though, that I encourage you to learn to have. It took me a long while to learn the art of balance. I want to help everyone, but in the end, we just can't. Sometimes, the burden of helping others became overwhelmingly heavy on my soul. When we give too much to others, we don't have anything left for ourselves. As wonderful as this job is, and though we possess strong emotional gifts that we want to use to help others, we must also help ourselves.

When I talk about help, there are two areas I think of. The first is helping your clients and understanding the important and beautiful role you play in others' lives. The second is helping yourself with regular self-care and hiring help so you can be the best of the best. I strongly believe it takes a team to be the best of the best in your area. When we ask for help and bring in key people to assist in the areas where we are weak, that is where the magic truly happens.

Running your own business is undoubtedly demanding, both physically and mentally. The emotional toll can be overwhelming as well. That's why it's essential to recognize the importance of asking for help and hiring assistance. While some entrepreneurs may strive to be a one-person show, taking on all tasks themselves, this approach can lead to burnout and even illness.

Learning to balance the stress of entrepreneurship is crucial for long-term success and personal well-being. As an entrepreneur, the drive to do everything yourself may be deeply ingrained in you. It took me years to find a balance and understand that running a business doesn't mean shouldering all the responsibilities alone. At one point, I considered my business my baby, and every success, failure, or setback weighed heavily on me. I took everything personally, and this emotional burden took a toll on my health.

When I was thirty-one, I was diagnosed with stage one breast cancer. I had been fighting for over seven months for a diagnosis. I just knew in my gut something wasn't right, and I could feel two hard lumps. My world flipped upside down. My four children were young, and I went from being able to do everything and being super independent to walking into what I call "cancer land." My life was soon filled with doctor appointments and surgeries.

After my bilateral mastectomy, I was overwhelmed by the love of my community. That diagnosis altered how I view life, money, and the value of my time.

Owning your own business comes with stress, and learning how to deal with it healthily is the key. I took on so much of my business emotionally and used to have panic attacks if a client was unhappy, or I would think about and obsess over my failures in the business rather than just putting on my big-girl panties and moving on.

Recognizing the need for help is a vital step in managing the demands of your business effectively. But what kind of help am I referring to? Let's consider the example of running a home daycare or preschool, where the hours can be exceedingly long. Once you achieve financial stability and have a full roster of clients, I strongly encourage you to bring on an assistant to help you run your program. This not only allows you to take much-needed breaks but also frees up your time to focus on other crucial aspects of your business. I would now rather make less money per month and have more freedom and time to do the things that absolutely bring me joy. We can't put a price tag on our time. It's invaluable and so very precious.

Throughout my journey, I found it invaluable to have a team of professionals supporting me. I hired a bookkeeper to manage my finances, an assistant to aid in the classroom, and a CPA to ensure my bookkeeping was accurate and up-to-date. As a dreamer and creative at heart, dealing with spreadsheets and meticulous financial tracking was not my forte. By delegating these responsibilities to experts in their respective fields, I could focus on my strengths and see the bigger picture of my business.

Expanding my preschool further emphasized the significance of seeking help. Trying to do it all myself, I was constantly overwhelmed and unable to keep up with the demands. However, as I began to hire more staff, such as additional teachers and a director, my business flourished and became financially stronger. The individuals I brought on board were experts in their roles, allowing me to rely on their expertise rather than attempting to master everything myself.

Remember, asking for help is not a sign of weakness or incompetence; it's an intelligent decision. Embracing assistance enables you to leverage the skills and knowledge of others, creating a more efficient and effective business. It empowers you to focus on your strengths and the aspects of the business that truly inspire you. By surrounding yourself with a capable team, you can cultivate a supportive environment that fosters growth and success.

Running a business can be an all-encompassing endeavor that takes a toll on your physical, mental, and emotional well-being. Recognizing the need for help and hiring assistance is not only vital for maintaining a healthy work-life balance but also for the growth and prosperity of your business. Don't hesitate to delegate tasks to experts, whether it's financial management, classroom assistance, or any other area where you need support. Embrace the brilliance of asking for help, and watch your business thrive.

Journal Prompt

What areas in your life feel stressful? How can you unburden yourself of some of that stress?

_____

_____

_____

_____

_____

_____

_____

_____

_____

_____

_____

_____

_____

_____

CHAPTER NINE

"I" is for Independence

"Independence is loyalty to one's best self and principles."
—Mark Twain

Being independent in the context of running your own business holds significant meaning. It's about standing out amidst the noise of the internet, social media, and the abundance of preschools and childcare centers surrounding you.

When I embarked on my journey in 2001, I was determined to establish myself as more than just another daycare. I wanted to be truly independent, offering a distinctive educational experience. In my mind, daycare was kind of like a glorified babysitter, and I aimed to be a school—a place where teaching and learning took center stage.

Starting out in my home, I made a deliberate choice to distance myself from the traditional home-based daycare model. I envisioned a professional establishment with a legitimate curriculum, regular newsletters, engaging art projects, and captivating bulletin boards. My goal was to create an environment that reflected a genuine school setting. Despite initially having only four children in my care, I saw myself as an independent and successful school from the outset. That's what I had envisioned, and I was moving forward knowing I would be an official preschool program with credibility. Remember, I was only twenty-three, and I had no idea how to run a business.

The internet was just a baby then. Do you remember when we had to dial up the internet? I just took what I had learned from my previous jobs and started to move forward with my little seed of an idea.

What I *did* know, even at that age with my limited knowledge, was that I was going to have to separate myself from the others. I needed to be different so I could fill up faster and start providing financially for my family. Being able to bring in my own money was important to me—I wanted to be an equal contributor alongside my husband.

As you embark on your own entrepreneurial journey, it's crucial to consider what independence means to you and your business. This is the time to turn your dreams into reality and shape your unique vision.

Start by understanding the needs of your community. Is there a demand for part-time or full-time care? Take the time to research and visit other programs in your area to gain insight into what they offer. Identify their strengths and weaknesses and use that knowledge to differentiate yourself and stand out. To truly be independent, you need to shine as an individual and as a business. Embrace your passions and allow them to guide your decision-making. What sets you apart? Are you passionate about science, art, or nature? Do you want to do an outdoor classroom? Or maybe you're passionate about cooking? Think about what brings you the greatest joy, and implement those elements into your program. Your passions will shine and make others excited about them, too.

When you figure out what makes your approach to early childhood education different and valuable, use these differentiating factors to shape your brand, marketing strategies, and overall business identity. Building a strong online presence, including a professional website and active social media engagement, can help you reach and attract the right audience. Remember, independence doesn't mean isolating yourself from others in the industry. Instead, it's about carving your own path and positioning yourself as a unique and valuable option for families seeking childcare and education. Cultivate a network of like-minded professionals, both within and outside the early childhood education field, who can support and inspire you on your journey. There are lots of Facebook group pages you can join to find a community of other childcare providers. In fact, I've created my own community where we inspire and encourage each other as early childhood educators. You can check it out and get more information on my website: thelovingstartway.com/community

Your independent business has the potential to thrive by offering something truly unique and meeting the specific needs of your community. As you continue to grow, nurture your vision and stay true to your core values. Regularly assess and refine your offerings to adapt to changing demands and emerging trends. Embracing independence means constantly evolving while staying true to your mission. It's about redefining the notion of daycare and establishing yourself as a school with a legitimate curriculum and a strong educational focus.

Researching your local market, understanding the needs of your community, and leveraging your unique strengths and passion will help you create a business that shines independently. Embrace your passions, develop your brand, and foster a network of support as you pave your own path to success.

Journal Prompt

How do you want to set yourself apart from other preschools in the area? What are you passionate about?

_____

_____

_____

_____

_____

_____

_____

_____

_____

_____

_____

_____

_____

_____

_____

CHAPTER TEN

"J" is for Juggling

*"Being strong means juggling sacrifices
while still pushing for progress."*
—Unknown

One of the most fun and rewarding aspects of the early childhood field is the ever-changing nature of each day. Every day brings newness, and no day will ever look the same. As educators, we come into our day with an outline, a curriculum, and a fun game plan. However, some days go right out the window because your little ones just aren't having it, or other days, the art project you thought would be amazing turns out to be a two-minute flop, or a project you thought would take ten minutes ends up taking thirty. When teaching early learners, even our best-laid plans rarely go as planned. But that's something I find truly amazing. After twenty-five years in the business, every day is still a surprise and never dull.

You get your steps in daily, and the time just flies in this business. Working with children means embarking on a new adventure every day. Their boundless energy, curiosity, and genuine joy for even the simplest things make them little balls of sunshine. It's no wonder I fell in love with this age group when I was just nineteen. In their eyes, the world is perfect, unburdened by prejudice or societal expectations. I love that they don't see color, sex, or religion. They are just full of joy and wonder. Childhood is a magical bubble, and it is our privilege to nurture and guide these young souls.

However, running a preschool or childcare center is a non-stop endeavor that requires exceptional juggling skills.

Every day presents a multitude of tasks and responsibilities, all while ensuring the happiness and safety of the children remains a top priority. It's a constant juggling act that demands attention and care.

Imagine feeding an infant while one of your toddlers starts to climb on the table, and another begins to cry because his friend just took his toy. Or maybe in your preschool class, you are in the middle of your morning art project, and you hear a little bright-eyed three-year-old girl who just had an accident crying in the corner. In this field, you'll find yourself racking up steps without ever setting foot in a gym. The fast pace of a preschool environment necessitates moving from one task to another with fluidity and grace—grace given to your students, your little ones, all day long in every given situation. You must have a lot of patience because our little ones need us to be the example of love and grace, and they must feel that they are okay no matter what happens that day.

From giving tours to prospective clients, changing diapers, feeding children, and putting them down for naps, you'll be simultaneously running the front office and managing administrative tasks. Juggling becomes second nature. To navigate this intricate dance of responsibilities, it's crucial to prioritize. Start by identifying the most pressing tasks—the "need-to-dos"—and tackle them first. Additionally, never lose sight of the fact that the needs of your students always come first. Their happiness, growth, and safety are paramount. By keeping their well-being at the forefront, you can ensure that your juggling remains focused on what truly matters.

Maintaining a consistent schedule within your center can be a valuable tool in finding balance and managing your tasks. Establishing routines helps create a sense of structure and predictability for both the children and you. It allows you to anticipate and plan for various needs, making your day flow more smoothly. As a result, time seems to fly by, and you become more adept at handling the myriad responsibilities that come your way.

Allow yourself the flexibility to let go of your schedule on occasion. If what the class needs is a little more play or outside time than you scheduled, it's okay; there is learning in all of it, from outside exploration to getting messy with shaving cream at the art table. Their minds are little sponges, learning every day, even in the simplest things. It's also so very important to remember that giving yourself grace is vital in this field. You may need to take them outside for fresh air just to catch your own breath.

Balancing office tasks and caring for young children can present challenges, and some days, it may take longer than expected to complete certain administrative duties. Working with young children means being flexible and adaptable. Embrace the reality that your juggling skills may take time to master, but with persistence, they will become a natural part of your routine.

As you embark on this journey, know that becoming a master juggler is a beautiful and rewarding process. Embrace the uniqueness of each day, cherish the wonder in the eyes of the children, and approach your tasks with grace and love. Your ability to juggle multiple responsibilities while nurturing young minds and hearts will shape the future of these children and make a lasting impact.

Juggling is an inherent part of running a preschool or childcare center. Prioritizing tasks and focusing on the needs of the children are crucial elements in mastering this delicate art. Embrace the fast-paced nature of the field, establish consistent schedules, and give yourself grace as you navigate the challenges. By juggling with grace and love, you will create a nurturing and thriving environment where children can blossom and grow.

Remember—you've got this: none of us are perfect, and learning to embrace the organized chaos is key to learning how to juggle with grace and love.

Journal Prompt

What are you currently juggling? What are some ideas that will help you juggle all the different areas of your new preschool?

CHAPTER ELEVEN

"K" Is for Kindness and Love

"In a world where so many are throwing bricks on others, be the one who builds bridges with them."
—Emma Xu

When running a preschool or childcare center, there are two values that stand above all others—kindness and love.

This chapter is of utmost importance, as it embodies the essence of what we do. While I may not be perfect and have made my fair share of mistakes, kindness and love have always been my guiding light in this business.

Over the years, I have seen employees who seem to dislike children come through my doors. They lacked love and kindness. It always surprises me, and I question why they spent time pursuing this career if they didn't have a passion for little ones. I strongly believe that love is the answer to everything and should be at the center of all that we do, both personally and professionally. When we put love as our center, we love others easily, and others can see the love within us, which can naturally attract people to us. If love is at the heart of everything you do in your business, your clients will see that and will trust you with their children.

To be in this field, a deep love for children is paramount. If that love doesn't flow within you, this may not be the right path for you. It astonishes me how often I encounter individuals who enter the teaching profession without genuinely liking or understanding young children.

Kindness and love are the foundation of success, not only in our work but in all aspects of life. For me, they are the answers to everything. Children crave and need kindness and love more than anything else. They thrive on hugs, reassurance, and constant support. As caretakers and educators, we have the privilege and responsibility of being their chosen guides from Monday through Friday. Our kindness, love, and respect for the little ones in our care nurture their souls, help cultivate a love for learning, and provide them with the security to grow and flourish.

Caring for young children is an incredibly beautiful gift, one that should never be taken lightly. You will form deep attachments to every student who comes through your doors, especially those who present challenges. It is these children who need our love and kindness the most, as they deserve every opportunity to succeed. With our unwavering love and kindness, we can witness even the most difficult children begin to thrive, and providing a safe space where they feel secure and loved is our responsibility.

When I originally named my business Smart Start Preschool, I thought of school and of "smart." We all want our kids to be successful when they grow up, right? As I continued to have more children, I quickly began to realize all four of them were wonderfully different. They needed me to parent differently, and they even had their own love languages. What worked for one didn't quite work for another.

Just recently, I went through a rebranding of my preschools. Over the past two decades of running my schools, the word *smart* wasn't really in my vocabulary, not with my own children or my students. I've never cared if they learned quickly or if my own kids got straight A's. Every student, every child learns differently and in their own time. I have always asked them just to do their best and honor and accept whatever their best is. What has been at the center of my teaching and parenting is love—loving my kids and my students just as they are and exactly where they are. So, after two decades, I decided to rebrand from the original Smart Start name to match what I've learned myself. And that's how Loving Start Learning Center was born because I believe that a Loving Start is a Smart Start.

When it comes time to build your team, it is vital to surround yourself with teachers who share your core values of kindness and love. You want a team that radiates love, unafraid to embrace a hurting child and shower them with affection. Your teachers should embody kindness in their interactions with students, parents, and fellow staff members.

Remember, kindness and love start with you as the leader. Your actions and attitudes set the tone for your entire team. Often, new parents place a disproportionate emphasis on academics, even planning their child's future college education when they are just one year old. There is so much pressure on our children today. Sometimes, as adults, we put all our hopes and wishes on our children, forgetting that they are on their own path, their own journey. I know that for a long time, I put a lot of pressure on myself as a mother. I felt I needed to be perfect and have the perfect children. That was exhausting and simply impossible. I'm not perfect, far from it, and neither are my kids. They have made horrible choices and done things that took my breath away, and all of it was what they were supposed to do. We want our kids to fail in the safety of our home so we can be there for them to help them pick up the pieces. We want to talk about failures openly and let them know that failures are part of life, part of growing, and in those failures, we can actually learn and become incredibly resilient.

As parents, we will fail over and over, and in our own failures, we can strive to be better. One of my favorite lines I came up with one day while talking to one of my kids was, "Just as you are learning to grow up, I am learning to be a good parent to you."

What if we take some pressure off our kids to be what we imagine them to be and take the pressure off ourselves to trust our kids are a representation of us? What if we can parent with love and grace, look at each of our children on their own journey, embrace that, and help facilitate getting them to their goals and dreams? In teaching, our role is to celebrate our students' uniqueness, not form them into a version of the students we want them to be.

Of course, let me be clear: I am a firm believer in rules, boundaries, and natural consequences. There are always consequences for our actions, whether good or bad. I'm not saying we should let our kids run wild. Children need and desire boundaries and guidelines. We should all expect our children to be kind and good human beings. But when it comes to academics, it's just not that simple. That's where we must be flexible and realize that not all children learn in one specific way. We also must not put our own dreams and wishes on them, defining what they should be when they grow up. It's their life, and they must eventually find their path just as we found ours.

I admit I may have fallen into the mindset of trying to mold my own children into my vision for them when they were young. However, over the years, I've come to understand that each child is beautifully unique. Looking back, I wish I had pulled two of my own kids from public school earlier in their formative years. I believe if they had been homeschooled, they would have flourished. If the way I taught them was different than the box public schools put our kids in, they may have been set up with so much more success.

Each child requires different forms of love and kindness. Academic success should never overshadow the central role that love plays in their growth and development. Beyond academics, kindness and love should permeate everything you do. When kindness and love become the driving force behind your actions, you will earn the respect of your students, their families, and the community at large. Your center will flourish, and your impact will endure for years to come. If you encounter a staff member who does not reflect the values of kindness and love, don't hesitate to address the issue. I, too, have made the mistake of prolonging necessary action, hoping for change. However, some individuals simply do not radiate love, and that's okay. But when kindness and love are at the center of your team, everything will fall into place.

I am a firm believer that kindness and love are the heart and soul of your business. Embrace the unique privilege of caring for and educating young children with boundless love and unwavering kindness. Cultivate a team that shares your values, create a safe and nurturing environment, and remember that academics should never overshadow the central role that love plays in a child's life. When kindness and love are the core of your business, you will witness the remarkable impact it has on your students and families.

Journal Prompt

What kind of work culture and school culture do you hope to create?

CHAPTER TWELVE

"L" is for Laws

"The laws are not to change the heart but to restrain the heartless."
—Martin Luther King Jr.

It is crucial to familiarize yourself with the laws and regulations that govern your operations. The safety and well-being of the children in your care should be your top priority, and adhering to the applicable laws is a fundamental aspect of providing a secure environment.

Remember, we are working with little humans, and their lives are precious. In order to have long-term success with your center, it is critical to follow the laws for safety as well as your city's and state's regulations for opening a center.

I have lived in California all my life, and I am quite familiar with Title 22—the Childcare Bible. It contains every state regulation for operating a home daycare and childcare center. As you move forward with your dream of opening a preschool, it's vital you do your homework regarding the laws centering around this industry. If you are going to run your business in your home, make sure you comply with any rules of your HOA or city. Most cities welcome home childcare, and there may be very few rules surrounding those unless you live in a neighborhood with an HOA. When you are opening a center, there are lots and lots of laws to follow. It's important to note that the specific laws and regulations vary from state to state and even from city to city. While I can offer insights into California's regulations, it's essential for you to research and understand the laws that apply to your location. You can research online, of course, or the best course of action would be to contact your local Community Care Licensing or the governing office that serves your county. They will be able to guide you through your state's regulations with orientations and webinars.

Start by conducting thorough research into your local zoning laws, as they may outline the requirements and restrictions for operating a childcare center. Familiarize yourself with the necessary permits, licenses, and certifications you must obtain. These may include zoning permits, health and safety inspections, fire safety clearances, and business licenses. Childcare centers are subject to a range of regulations regarding staff qualifications, child-to-staff ratios, background checks, and health and safety standards. Educate yourself on these regulations to ensure compliance and the highest level of care for the children in your program. It is illegal to simply open a childcare facility, whether in your home or in a center, without the proper licenses.

In addition to local regulations, you must also adhere to state-specific laws. These laws typically cover areas such as curriculum requirements, immunization records, emergency preparedness plans, and reporting procedures for accidents or incidents. Stay updated on any changes to these laws and ensure that your center remains in compliance. Maintaining compliance with laws and regulations can be complex and time-consuming, but it is essential for the success and reputation of your business.

Consider consulting with an attorney or a local agency that specializes in childcare regulations to ensure you have a thorough understanding of the legal requirements. Remember, laws exist to protect the well-being of the children in your care. Embracing compliance not only demonstrates your commitment to their safety but also instills confidence in parents and the community. By following the laws and regulations, you can build a strong foundation for your business and provide a nurturing and secure environment for the children you serve. Take a deep breath and approach each step of the process one at a time. While it may seem overwhelming, remember that compliance with laws is a crucial aspect of your business journey.

Stay informed, seek guidance when needed, and prioritize the safety and well-being of the children above all else.

Sample Checklist for Opening a Preschool: Ensuring Compliance with Laws and Regulations

1. *Check your local zoning*: Research and understand the zoning laws and restrictions in your area to determine if operating a preschool or childcare center from your home or a commercial building is allowed.

2. *Visit your state childcare website*: Explore your state's childcare licensing website, such as California's Community Care Licensing, for step-by-step instructions and guidelines on opening a home-based school or center. Familiarize yourself with the requirements and procedures specific to your state.

3. *Fill out necessary applications:* Complete all required applications, forms, and paperwork as outlined by your state's childcare licensing agency. For a home-based school, you may need to attend an orientation, obtain CPR/first aid certification, and complete online webinars on safety. A state visit is usually conducted to approve your home as a suitable environment for childcare.

4. *Apply as a commercial center, if applicable:* If you are planning to open a center in a commercial building, the application process may be more extensive. Find an appropriate commercial space and work with your city's zoning department to ensure compliance. You will need a qualified director, teachers, and comprehensive marketing

materials as part of your application. A fire marshal will also inspect the premises for safety compliance.

5. *Set up state and city visits:* Arrange for the necessary visits from state and city officials to inspect your facility and ensure compliance with regulations. These visits may include inspections of the physical space, documentation review, and verification of staff qualifications.

6. *Obtain required certifications:* Depending on your state's regulations, ensure that you and your staff obtain the necessary certifications, such as CPR/first aid training, background checks, and health screenings.

7. *Complete the licensing process:* Once all visits and inspections are successfully completed, and all requirements are met, you can proceed with the licensing process. This will grant you official permission to operate your preschool or childcare center.

8. *Keep and maintain good records at your preschool:* Most states require files on your students with the appropriate state forms. File keeping is vital for the success of your business.

Remember, this sample checklist is intended to provide a general overview, and the specific requirements may vary depending on your state and city. Conduct thorough research, consult with local authorities, and carefully follow the guidelines provided by your state's childcare licensing agency.

While the process may seem overwhelming, take it step by step and remain organized. Keep in mind that compliance with laws and regulations ensures the safety and well-being of the children in your care. With diligence and patience, you can navigate the necessary steps to open a preschool that meets all legal requirements and provides a nurturing environment for children to learn and grow.

Journal Prompt

Make a list of local and state laws you may need to check on, depending on what kind of building you want to operate your school in.

CHAPTER THIRTEEN

"M" is for Money

"Chase the vision, not the money. The money will end up following you."
—Tony Hsieh

Let's talk about money! While there are numerous outstanding male professionals in the childcare field, the majority are women. As women, we sometimes shy away from discussing money, but my hope is that you can take pride in your financial contributions and feel comfortable engaging in this conversation. Whatever your reason is for wanting to open your own preschool, I'm sure money is part of it. It has to be because in order to run a successful business, you must make a profit. If you don't, well, I don't have to tell you that your business will be in trouble.

You will be working hard, and you should be paid for your talent and effort.

In this chapter, we will discuss the financial aspect of running a preschool or childcare center. It is important to remember that while financial stability is a goal, the primary driving force should be a passion for service and making a positive impact on children, families, and the community.

I believe when you are passionate and have a wonderful, high-quality program, you will benefit by making a good profit.

When starting a preschool, researching the prices of other schools in the area can help determine an appropriate pricing strategy. Starting with lower prices initially can be helpful for attracting new families. However, building a sustainable income takes time and may not be immediate. The following is a sample budgeting approach that can be customized to fit your specific circumstances:

Sample Home-Based Model Budget:

Licensed for 12 students

Full-time rate: $1,200 per child

Gross income: $14,400

Expenses:

    Teacher: $3,200

    Food (if applicable): $1,000 (parents bringing their own)

    Bookkeeper: $60

    Phone: $75

    Supplies: $700

    Insurance/workers' compensation: $300

    Office: $200

Net income: $8,865

Medium Center Sample Budget:

Licensed for 48 students (mix of full-time and part-time)

Gross income: $40,000

Expenses:

    Rent: $3,500

    Utilities: $1,000 (varies based on the building and time of year)

    Payroll for a team of 6 (overstaffing for coverage): $20,000

    Supplies: $1,500

    Insurance/workers' compensation: $350

    Office: $1,200

    Landscape: $150

    Events: $600 (regularly hosting events for families)

    Teacher gifts/team building: $300

Net income: $11,400 (sample numbers only)

Remember that these are just sample budgets, and the actual numbers will vary based on your location, rates, and specific expenses. It's crucial to carefully analyze your income and expenses and adjust accordingly. I am in California, so the pricing may be higher than in your home state.

These are just samples of potential income that can be made. Maintaining financial stability requires setting budgets, managing expenses, and projecting your finances year to year. It is important to prioritize the needs of your students and staff, as they should come before personal financial gain. I have always paid my staff first, then myself. Some may say you must pay yourself first, but I have never wavered on my stance that my team is first, then myself. While owning a preschool can provide financial stability, it is not a guaranteed path to wealth. However, it can offer a decent income and the satisfaction of contributing to your family's budget or achieving personal financial independence.

By leading with love, kindness, and a focus on service, your preschool will naturally attract clients, allowing you to charge competitive rates and create a steady income for the long term. Remember that finding a balance between financial sustainability and providing quality care is key. Regularly review your budget, explore opportunities for growth, and ensure that your spending aligns with the needs of your students and staff. By maintaining a focus on service and financial responsibility, your preschool can thrive and continue to make a positive impact on the lives of children, families, and your community. Before you know it, you will be your own "boss babe" with your own income, giving you the freedom to live the life you've always imagined.

Journal Prompt

How does money make you feel? What areas in your life can be improved with the possibility of opening your own preschool?

_____

_____

_____

_____

_____

_____

_____

_____

_____

_____

_____

_____

_____

_____

CHAPTER FOURTEEN

"N" is for No

"It's only by saying NO that you can concentrate on the things that are really important."
—Steve Jobs

In this chapter, we will discuss the importance of saying "no" and setting boundaries in the preschool business.

As educators and natural givers, it can be challenging to prioritize ourselves and establish limits. However, learning the art of saying "no" without guilt is crucial for maintaining a healthy and successful preschool environment. In this business, children bring joy, but sometimes parents can present challenges, and you will have to make the hard decisions for the betterment of your school. It's not easy, believe me. I've had many sleepless nights over the years stressing about students, parents, and staff. I have been rather slow over the years to let go of the people who bring down others or who bring stress into my life. I have always wanted to see the best in everyone. I will listen, hear their story, and try to believe in the power of change, but sometimes there is no change; some people just live their lives with drama and negativity all the time. No matter how many pep talks or chances you may give, the patterns remain.

I wish I had learned the art of "no" earlier in my life, both personally and professionally. Just because my natural instinct is to want to see the best in people doesn't mean I have to accept their patterns of negativity. It's okay to release them, and it's okay to have boundaries with your happiness. I've had to learn the hard way both in my first marriage and with staff over the years who brought my team down. I wholeheartedly believe in second and third chances and listening with grace and kindness, but what I wish I had done sooner for myself was recognize the people around me personally and professionally who weren't changing and would never change. I wish I learned the art of protecting my personal boundaries sooner. But once I did learn, my life has been abundantly happier and more peaceful. I have the life now that I once only dreamed of having, and it still amazes me.

Sometimes, you have to let a difficult child go, and it's never easy. We want to help them all, but sometimes we aren't equipped, and after multiple conferences and different strategies, it's okay to say, "I'm sorry, but I think it's time to find another school." This goes for parents at your school as well. Just recently, we had to let go of a client because they made many of our team members feel uncomfortable with demeaning and inappropriate sexual comments. My goal with these hard decisions is always to consider what is best for my business and my team. In your personal life, make decisions on the basis of your joy. Ask yourself, *Does this bring me joy?*

Managing all the different aspects of running a preschool can be overwhelming, so it's essential to recognize that not every situation or individual is a good fit for your program. I recall a personal experience where a parent consistently brought negativity into my classroom. Despite my passion and dedication to creating a positive learning environment, this parent's constant complaints would burst my bubble. After two years of successfully running my home school and having a waitlist, I made the difficult decision to let her go. I handed her a refund of her tuition for the month and explained that her negativity was not working out. By saying "no" to her and setting a boundary, I prioritized my own well-being and the overall good of my school. Guess what happened? She begged me to stay and was never negative again.

In this business, you may encounter difficult children or challenging parents. While children can often be guided with kindness and love, the parents may pose a greater challenge. Remember that providing excellent customer service means customizing each client's experience, but it also means considering what is best for your school and yourself. It is crucial to prioritize self-care and set boundaries in order to run a successful preschool. Saying no to situations or individuals that do not serve your well-being or the overall good of your program is healthy and necessary. As women, who often dominate this field, we may have a natural inclination to please others. However, to be good parents and business owners, we must first take care of ourselves.

If you find yourself strapped for money or tempted to compromise your boundaries due to financial pressures, it's important to remember the long-term stability and health of your business. Setting clear boundaries and saying no when necessary will ultimately contribute to a healthier and more sustainable environment. Learning to say no and establishing boundaries is an ongoing process. It may take time to overcome the guilt or discomfort associated with it, but it is an essential skill for maintaining your well-being and the success of your preschool. By prioritizing self-care, setting boundaries, and saying no when needed, you create a stable and positive environment for yourself, your staff, and the children in your care. Remember that your own well-being is just as important as the well-being of your clients. If you are not the best version of yourself, it's hard to sell yourself to others. I believe that no can be an act of self-love and self-preservation.

Journal Prompt

What areas in your life are not serving you well? What do you want your life to look like? What brings you joy?

_____

_____

_____

_____

_____

_____

_____

_____

_____

_____

_____

_____

_____

_____

CHAPTER FIFTEEN

"O" Is for Operations

> *"In the end, all business operations can be reduced to three words: people, product, and profits."*
> —Lee Iacocca

Business operations are a huge part of the business's long-term success. *Operations* is a broad term, and, honestly, it will grow bigger and more detailed as your business grows.

When I first started, I had a vision in my head: I had a schedule I wanted for teaching my students. I envisioned circle time, art time, outside time, snack time, and music and movement. I knew I wanted to create a monthly newsletter, and since I wanted to be looked at differently from my peers, I wanted to have marketing materials that showcased my school. That is how I started; that was as far as my operations went. It wasn't until I started to really grow that I realized operations was bigger than my daily schedule and my monthly newsletter.

So before we dive in, if you plan to start off small, you really won't need too much in this department. Once you bring on an assistant, your operations will grow a little more detailed because then you will be in charge of training your assistant on how your program operates. When you are a one-person show, your operations can be quite simple. Your focus will be mostly on your day-to-day procedures for your clients, so they have a clear understanding of what is expected of them and what they can expect of you. When you bring others on, you will need to get your operations dialed in.

In this chapter, we will explore the significance of operations in the preschool business. How you operate and present yourself can make a significant difference in how parents and potential clients perceive you. Having a detailed and well-thought-out plan is crucial for establishing professionalism and standing out in a competitive market. When starting out, it's important to create a written plan for every aspect of your preschool. Even as a home-based educator, having clear guidelines and procedures will set you apart. When you eventually get licensed for a center, you will need handbooks, admission agreements, and various documents concerning your school. Starting with these materials demonstrates to your clients that you have taken the time to establish comprehensive operational systems. Your tour packet, which provides information and pricing for parents to keep after they tour your facility, is a valuable marketing tool.

In today's digital age, it's essential to have a strong online presence and effective branding. Designing a logo, tagline, and website will enhance your professionalism. Business social media pages, such as Facebook, Instagram, and TikTok, can also be powerful marketing tools. However, always remember to obtain permission from parents before featuring children's faces in your marketing material.

When it comes to creating marketing materials and documents, there are various user-friendly apps and platforms available. Canva is a popular app that allows you to easily create visually appealing marketing materials. Fiverr is another resource where you can find independent contractors who can help with tasks like designing logos or managing your social media.

Presenting yourself professionally and demonstrating how your school operates is crucial for attracting clients. It's not enough to have a vision in your head; you must write it down and present it to your prospective clients. The following are key items that should be included in your tour packet and highlight your operations:

- **Parent handbook:** This comprehensive guide covers your school's philosophy, mission statement, sample daily schedule, food policy, illness and emergency protocols, clothing guidelines, what to bring on the first day, closure policies, and more. It serves as a reference for all policies and procedures.

- **Calendar:** Provide a yearly calendar at the beginning of each year, outlining all closure dates so parents can plan accordingly. This helps avoid surprises or last-minute changes.

- **Pricing, hours, and class schedules:** Clearly outline your pricing structure, including registration and material fees, along with the hours and class schedules you offer.

- **Admission agreement:** This is a summary of your handbook that parents will sign and date, ensuring that everyone is on the same page regarding expectations.

When you begin bringing in your team, your operations materials will expand. Here are a few things I use when onboarding my team:

- **Staff handbook:** This is a guidebook for team members regarding policies, procedures, team philosophy, and what is expected from them. Make sure it's clear and presented clearly so you set your team members up for success in your business.

- **Job description:** This is a clearly defined job description that lists job requirements, education, CPR/first aid requirements, and classroom management expectations, with all things clearly detailed to provide a clear understanding of what is required of them daily.

Operations play a vital role in the success of your preschool. By being organized, professional, and transparent in your operations, you establish clear boundaries and expectations for both yourself and your clients. Clients who resonate with your philosophy will be drawn to your program, while those who do not will move on. Taking the time to create thorough and well-presented operational material is a valuable investment in your business and is vital for leading your team members, whether you have one or twenty-five. Providing written policies and procedures creates a unified team and clearly defined expectations for everyone. So start taking notes, organizing your thoughts, and crafting your operational documents. Enjoy the process and take your time, as this is essential and valuable work that will contribute to the long-term success of your preschool.

Journal Prompt

What are some of your "must-haves" in your day-to-day operations? What are the basics you want to include?

CHAPTER SIXTEEN

"P" Is for Philosophy

> *"Be the change you wish to see in the world."*
> —Mahatma Gandhi

When opening a preschool, one question you are likely to encounter is, "What is your teaching philosophy?" I promise you will get this question a lot. This is one of the fun parts of creating your own preschool. We talked earlier about passions. This is where you can implement all the things that bring you joy. Think of your philosophy as the heartbeat of your center. Developing a clear philosophy is essential in the field of early childhood education.

While it is beneficial to take basic early childhood education classes to gain knowledge and understanding, it is not required. However, I highly, *highly* recommend that you take the classes, even if you will be running your business in your home. You know the saying, "Knowledge is power." It is so important to understand the why of what we do as early childhood educators. If you haven't taken the classes, you may not understand all the learning these amazing little humans truly can take on. The growth from zero to five years old is incredible, and their potential is great.

In the realm of early childhood education, there are numerous philosophies that have stood the test of time. Some notable ones include the

Montessori approach, Waldorf education, the Reggio Emilia approach, and play-based philosophy. Let's explore each briefly:

- **Montessori**: Developed by Maria Montessori, the Montessori method is both a philosophy and a teaching method. It is based on the belief that children possess a natural desire to learn and can excel when placed in an enriched environment with specially designed materials and trained teachers. The approach emphasizes hands-on experiences and encompasses various areas of development, including self-care, math, language, cultural studies, and more.

- **Waldorf:** Rooted in the ideals and methods of Rudolf Steiner, Waldorf education aims to support the development of free-thinking, self-directed individuals. It places a strong emphasis on imagination and play, with a focus on using simple, natural materials to encourage children to engage in creative thinking, problem-solving, and social skill development.

- **Reggio Emilia approach:** Originating from the schools of Reggio Emilia in Italy, this approach highlights the arts as children's symbolic language and focuses on creating an engaging learning environment. Collaboration among teachers, parents, children, and the community is a key aspect, with parents being considered equal partners in their children's education.

- **Play-based philosophy:** Recognizing that play is a fundamental aspect of a child's development, this philosophy emphasizes the importance of purposeful play. It encourages children to think creatively, develop problem-solving abilities, and foster social, emotional, and physical growth. Play is viewed as a way of learning and is incorporated into the daily routines of a high-quality early childhood program.

As an educator, you have the freedom to shape your own teaching philosophy and establish your school's approach. Reflecting on your experiences and values can help you create a unique philosophy that resonates with you and the children you serve. Drawing inspiration from different philosophies and incorporating various elements that align with your beliefs can create a well-rounded and inclusive approach to early education.

In your own philosophy, you may prioritize the importance of love and nurturing at the core while embracing elements from different philosophies such as play, academics, nature-based learning, and individualized instruction. The Loving Start Way, my personal philosophy, combines the best aspects of multiple philosophies to cater to the unique needs and interests of each child. This approach allows you to see every student as special and adapt your teaching strategies accordingly. Remember earlier when I talked about my own children being wonderfully different from each other? Each of them learned and processed life differently, and now, as adults, each is on their own path, pursuing their own goals and dreams. The same goes for your future students.

In my centers, I've adapted some of all the philosophies to serve every child who walks through my doors. The Loving Start Way has love as the center and celebrates our students and their uniqueness first and foremost through a creative, hands-on curriculum. Creating your own school philosophy is an exciting part of establishing your preschool. It allows you to craft an approach that reflects your values and teaching style and the needs of the children you serve. Remember, there is no one-size-fits-all philosophy, and the beauty of starting your own school lies in the freedom to shape and personalize it to suit your vision and the needs of your students. Enjoy the process of creating your unique philosophy and embracing the joy of making your school truly yours.

Journal Prompt

What philosophy do you want to use in your program? What are your core beliefs?

CHAPTER SEVENTEEN

"Q" Is for Quiet

"Silence is a source of great strength."
—Lao Tzu

In the busy and often hectic world of working with children, it is crucial to recognize the value of quiet moments.

As an educator, you give your all each day, and it's natural to feel exhausted by the end of it. Incorporating quiet time into your program, including nap or rest time, is essential for the children and yourself. We live in a fast-paced and information-overloaded society today. If we feel this, imagine our children being raised in the hustle and bustle. More than ever, we have so much noise on a daily basis and have to sort through technology and the media and our busy, hectic schedules. It can be easy to feel lost, overwhelmed, and emotionally and physically exhausted.

For a long time, I could never just sit and be. I thought it was being lazy if I just sat on the couch for an extended period of time. How ridiculous, right? When I was raising my four amazing humans, I was constantly on the go, running from the time I woke up until nine at night when I absolutely crashed into bed. I had the daily routines of school and work, taking them from one practice to another, to dinner, homework, and bedtime, well, you get it. I somehow was misguided along the way and correlated my worth to my being busy.

So many times a week, I would hear, "I don't know how you do it, juggling it all." Looking back, I realize now that comment made me feel good; it was part of my worth as a human. But now, even as I write this, I am shaking my head.

Along the way, I interpreted love as checking off a box of things to do and accomplish. I also used being busy as my coping mechanism. I was addicted to being busy. If I was busy, I couldn't feel my emotions or sit in the pain of an emotionally abusive marriage. By constantly hustling and engaging in volunteering, humanitarian work, parenting, and my job, I didn't have time to stop and realize that I was wearing a mask, hiding my deep unhappiness with my marriage. So, my coping skill was to ignore it.

Eventually, that caught up when I was diagnosed with breast cancer at thirty-one. I believe in my heart that because I was living in fight or flight for most of my adult life, my immune system wore down. My stress from an unhealthy marriage and not knowing how to set good boundaries in business may have been part of why I got breast cancer so young.

A few years ago, after my divorce and after lots of therapy and work on myself, I took a one-year sabbatical. It was in August of 2019. For the first time since 2001, I was going to not work in my business. I had grown my business and had a fully capable and amazing team to lead my schools. It was the first time that I was going to step back and let my team handle everything. I had been on my own since 2015, and with work and the kids, I never truly healed, and found myself repeating patterns and allowing others into my life who were unstable. I had to take a deep dive into myself to see my role in all of this, take ownership, and truly heal.

I think sometimes the universe keeps giving us the same problems and situations until we actually learn the lessons it's trying to teach us. After a month of therapy, energy work, and lots of writing, I began to identify my addiction to being busy and started to feel all that was bottled up for so long. As hard, ugly, and raw as it was, it truly was a gift.

You know those moments when you're rolled up in a ball on the bathroom floor, unsure if you can make it another day? I had many of those. It took me ten years to make the decision to leave my marriage—the only person I loved for seventeen years. Being the one who pursued the divorce left me with an enormous amount of guilt that I had ruined my kids and the family unit they knew and loved.

But in 2019, I decided to take some time off and truly heal and enjoy life and learn that I could be loved without accomplishing, without being busy. I was kicking my coping skills to the curb once and for all. It was truly extraordinary. I learned to sit on my couch and just be still—no talking, no music, just listening to the birds singing outside. I learned not to feel guilty for lying on my couch for a day and watching Netflix. I learned to have no schedule at all some days, and most of all, I fell in love again with the most amazing man during this time. He is the love of my life, truly. I now can say I have experienced true love, and I don't take our love or our marriage lightly; it's a wonderful gift I cherish.

All of these beautiful blessings came out of me being still and taking time for myself—taking the time to feel my pain, get clarity on my future, and understand that it's absolutely okay to sit on the couch and do nothing at all. I firmly believe that all the answers to our questions are inside of us, but we have to be still and quiet the noise around us.

I encourage you to practice stillness, especially when you are a business owner. Situations will arise that will require you to make tough decisions. That year's sabbatical turned into almost four years. I have learned to trust my team, and they have done an even better job than I could ever do.

Just as we need rest and quiet, so do our little ones. When creating your preschool program, remember to provide an opportunity for all students to rest. While younger children require nap time for their health and growth, older students may outgrow the need for a nap but still benefit from a quiet period. You can encourage older children to engage in quiet activities after a designated resting period. Turning off the lights, playing soft music, and creating a peaceful environment contribute to a tranquil atmosphere that benefits both children and adults. Quieting the mind and body is not only beneficial for children but also for you as an educator and business owner.

In the midst of your busy schedule, it is important to find moments of stillness and solitude. Allowing yourself to pause, breathe, and reflect can bring a sense of peace and clarity. In many cases, running a business and juggling multiple responsibilities can lead to feeling overwhelmed by the noise and demands of everyday life. By intentionally setting aside personal time for quiet and stillness, you can clear the mental clutter and gain clarity when making significant decisions in your business and personal life. Embracing moments of silence and serenity can provide the mental and emotional space necessary for self-care and rejuvenation.

Based on my experience, I've learned it is crucial to recognize the dangers of constantly running at full speed without incorporating moments of quiet and stillness. Over time, the toll of perpetual busyness can catch up to us, resulting in burnout and detrimental effects on our well-being. It is important to acknowledge that perfection is an unattainable goal and that it's okay to make mistakes. Understanding your limitations and prioritizing self-care is essential for long-term success and fulfillment.

As a preschool owner, it is your responsibility to create an environment of positivity and joy. However, this begins with cultivating those qualities within yourself. Recognize that you are a rock star for working with young children and bringing enthusiasm to your center. But to sustain your energy and enthusiasm, you must prioritize moments of quiet and self-reflection. Learn from the mistakes of others and me, and avoid the pitfalls of taking on too much and internalizing stress. Compartmentalizing your role in the business, finding peace in imperfection, and practicing self-compassion are invaluable lessons.

By incorporating stillness into your life, you can achieve a deeper level of clarity and make sound decisions for yourself and your business. Remember, just as you provide quiet and rest time for your students, you must also prioritize self-care and personal moments of tranquility. By doing so, you ensure your long-term success and well-being as an educator and business owner and can avoid burnout. Embrace the power of quiet and discover the strength and clarity it brings to your life.

Journal Prompt

What are the areas in your life that cause stress? What can help you prioritize a quiet time every day for yourself?

CHAPTER EIGHTEEN

"R" is for Research

"Research is formalized curiosity. It is poking and prying with a purpose."
—Zora Neale Hurston

As you embark on your journey to open your own preschool, conducting thorough research becomes essential for setting yourself up for success. Researching your competitors and the area in which you plan to operate is a crucial step in understanding the market and identifying opportunities to stand out. This is the perfect time to hone your spying skills.

When you are established and running your own school, the tables will be turned, and you will then be spied on. It's vital to research your competitors, especially when it comes to pricing your program.

To begin, gather information about the existing schools and home-based providers in your area. There's no shame in being curious and exploring other centers. In fact, it's beneficial to gain firsthand knowledge of your competition. Send members of your management team to tour different schools, observing their strengths, weaknesses, and overall atmosphere. In fact, go out by yourself and visit different schools. I am telling you—you will learn so much. Think of it as your first field trip in the business. You will see things you'll love and other things you'll despise. You may need to call ahead of time and make appointments or just do drop-in tours. While you are there, pay attention to details such as the cleanliness, scent, and overall first impression. Remember, our senses play a significant role in shaping our experiences, even if we're not consciously aware of it.

By conducting research and understanding the competition, you'll gain valuable insight that will help you position your preschool uniquely. Consider what is missing in the area and how your school can fill that gap.

Additionally, researching the market will aid in determining appropriate tuition prices. Just as you would when selling a house, you should set your prices based on how you compare to others in the surrounding market. Strive to find a balance between affordability for families and fair compensation for your services. Remember, if your prices are too high, you may have a hard time filling up. If you are too low, you may be leaving money on the table. It's a delicate thing to set your tuition prices. Always remember if you do set them and they aren't working, maybe they are too high; there is no shame in lowering them. It is trickier to raise them once your clients are enrolled.

Whether you plan to operate from your home or establish a center, it's important to visit and explore similar facilities. Tour at least five or six home preschools or centers, collecting information and tour packets for research purposes. This information is intended to provide you with insight into what is working well in your area and to help you create your own unique program.

IMPORTANT NOTE: it is crucial to maintain your integrity and avoid copying others' materials or programs.

Even if you have years of experience, continuous research is vital. Consider taking early childhood education classes to deepen your understanding of child development and best practices. These courses will provide you with valuable insight into the growth and development of children aged 0-5. It's important to stay knowledgeable about the field you're entering and ensure that you can confidently represent and sell your program to prospective families.

Speaking of selling, remember that when conducting tours and showcasing your program to potential clients, you are not only promoting your preschool but also selling yourself. Approach these interactions with the intention of connecting with families and conveying your genuine passion and commitment to education. First impressions matter, and showcasing your philosophy and values will help families understand if your program aligns with their needs. If your school is not the right fit for a family, be honest and recommend alternative options that may better suit their requirements. Building a strong connection and rapport with families is key to creating a thriving community.

Finally, keep in mind that education and research are ongoing processes. The field of early childhood education is ever-evolving, and staying up-to-date with current research and trends is crucial. By investing time and effort into conducting thorough research, you set yourself up for long-term success and ensure that your program remains relevant and effective. It's also good not to make this research a one-time thing. Every couple of years, go tour other schools just to help keep your own program relevant.

Remember, research provides the foundation upon which you can build your preschool. By gaining insight into your competitors, understanding the market, and continuously educating yourself, you create a solid framework that will support the growth and development of your program over time.

Journal Prompt

What are the five schools in your area you want to visit? After your visit, what are some things you loved and some you hated?

CHAPTER NINETEEN

"S" is for Schedules

*"The key is not to prioritize what's on your schedule
but to schedule your priorities."*
—Stephen Covey

Creating and maintaining a clear schedule is essential for a well-organized and successful preschool program, whether you operate from your home or a center. Schedules provide structure, routine, and predictability for children, promoting a sense of security and reducing stress.

Let's delve into the importance of schedules and how they can contribute to the smooth operation of your program.

Recently, I acquired a new school. It was unexpected, and I wasn't planning on opening another school. But sometimes, opportunity comes knocking, and it's up to us to say yes and see what can happen next. This Montessori school had been operating for the past seventeen years, and I converted it into my own Loving Start program. It had been six years since I last opened a school, and this new school presented a few challenges I was eager to conquer. One challenge was that the school consisted of one large room, including a sectioned-off infant program with low walls and its own nap room. When I first walked in, it felt so homey and absolutely adorable. However, this was the first time since 2010 that I was going to run a school in one room with all the different ages. I quickly realized this was going to be harder than expected. What I liked about it was it felt like my home version but on a bigger scale. However, when you put the bigger scale into play, we are talking twenty-four kids versus twelve kids, which can be challenging.

I took over in December, and two of the biggest issues were the schedule and the mixed ages. The school had been struggling, so I started with only a handful of students. But soon, I had doubled the enrollment. Changing a program into your own in an acquisition is a bit of a dance and balancing act. The issues were the schedule and separating our younger students from the older ones, so all of our students were getting what they needed academics-wise. I installed a small, gated area, creating a two-year-old class, and then quickly did it again to create another designated space.

But the school was struggling with its schedule, or lack thereof. I had perfected my daily schedule over two decades, but for some reason, this particular location just couldn't seem to get it together regarding our routine. Possibly, the one-room setup presented more issues than I had anticipated. Usually, my schools have individual classrooms with a teacher who is specifically in charge of that group. This new school felt like more of a team effort with a lack of one designated person to really take the lead and actually teach. We needed to get creative to solve our schedule issues, and we continually tweaked the schedule, such as having our two-year-olds outside while the older ones were in circle time.

You also have to have the right staff in order to be successful. Part of our issues, I believe, came from the fact that the staff I had hired was lacking in classroom management, so we had to do some intense training. It took three months to dial in the daily schedule at this school, the longest ever. It really reminded me how vital a daily schedule and routine is. A lack of routine creates chaos. Now, a preschool environment is controlled chaos on most days, but a lack of classroom management or lack of consistent schedules creates a lot of unwanted stress and chaos.

Little ones need reliability, consistency, and schedules to thrive. When they know what comes next, it offers them a feeling of safety. When you establish a schedule, it's crucial for you and your team to adhere to it consistently. Deviations from the schedule can disrupt the flow and create chaos, causing unnecessary stress. Having a shared understanding and commitment to following the schedule is key to maintaining order within your program.

I felt like a broken record drilling in this simple thought of a schedule with my new team. What is hard with a startup is that sometimes it takes a minute to find the right team members. In that process, there is a lot of change and moving around team members as you learn their gifts and what age group they shine the best with. This is also a time when you must be quick to let go or fire a team member if they do not match your philosophy. Rip the Band-Aid off quickly rather than slowly; it's better for all involved.

To illustrate the significance of schedules, let's take a look at the real-life example of this school. This one-room school was a converted Ace Hardware store. While the building had a charming and cozy feel reminiscent of my early years running a home-based preschool, it presented challenges in terms of limited class space and schedule coordination. The school had separate spaces for infants and preschoolers, with the infant program running smoothly from the beginning. However, accommodating different age groups within the preschool side proved to be more challenging. Initially, I implemented a standard schedule for my Loving Start program and created partitioned areas within the large room to create age-appropriate class spaces. However, the transition was not without bumps along the way. One important lesson I learned during this process was the critical role of assembling the right team. When running a larger center, having dedicated and passionate staff who align with your philosophy and program is essential. It's necessary to find individuals who genuinely care about early education and are committed to following the schedule, implementing the curriculum, and maintaining a positive learning environment. While it may take time to find the right team members, it's important not to settle for individuals who do not share your vision, as they can create disruptions and challenges within your program.

Children thrive on routine and knowing what to expect next. A well-structured program with a consistent daily schedule helps children feel secure and engaged. It also allows for smoother transitions between activities and minimizes behavior issues that may arise from boredom or unpredictability. Remember, a schedule is not meant to be rigid but is rather a framework that provides a sense of order while allowing for flexibility and individualized learning experiences.

When you are starting up, remember that sometimes it's not easy. Most times, the beginning takes adjusting. Just like every fall when you have a new class to teach and it takes a few weeks to get to know the kids' personalities and skill levels, there are always bumps in the road when initially establishing your routine and schedule. Don't give up; have some patience, and keep trying. It will begin to fall into place, and you will find being consistent in your schedule will create peace in the classroom and less chaos.

Here is an example of the Loving Start daily schedule:

7:00 a.m.–8:30 a.m.: Before Care
8:30 a.m.: Welcome to class, Free Time, Art Time
9:00 a.m.: Morning Circle Time
9:20 a.m.: Learning Centers (Academics, Art, Science, Math)
10:15 a.m.: Snack
10:30 a.m.: Outside Exploration
11:30 a.m.: Closing Circle Time
11:45 a.m.: Morning children go home
12:00 p.m.: Lunch
12:40 p.m.: Quiet Time/Rest Time
1:30 p.m.: Resters engage in quiet activities
2:30 p.m.: All children awake
2:40 p.m.: Closing Circle Time
3:00 p.m.–5:30 p.m.: After Care

When I first started my home-based preschool, I operated part-time, offering morning and afternoon classes on specific days. As my children grew up, I expanded to a larger building and offered extended hours with before- and after-school care.

The schedule you choose should align with the needs of your community, whether it's infant care, extended days, or part-time options. Conducting thorough research on the demand in your area will help you determine the most suitable schedule and classes to offer.

A well-planned daily routine provides structure and helps you manage the various aspects of your program effectively. It allows you to identify when you need extra support during transitions and when it's more suitable for giving tours or engaging in quieter activities. Remember, schedules bring structure, routine, and joy to your program. They provide children with a sense of security, promote smoother transitions, and create a positive learning environment. By assembling a dedicated team that shares your vision and adheres to a consistent schedule, you can establish a thriving and successful preschool.

Journal Prompt

What does your daily schedule look like?

CHAPTER TWENTY

"T" is for Training

"The beautiful thing about learning is that nobody can take it away from you."
—B.B. King

Training is a vital aspect of running a successful preschool. While formal education and degrees can be valuable, what truly matters in this field is the passion, dedication, and drive to make a positive impact on young children's lives. As an owner, it's essential to understand the regulations and expectations set by your state and city, ensuring compliance with licensing requirements.

Training encompasses various areas, including understanding the stages of growth and learning in early childhood. The years from 0 to 5 are critical for children's development, and being knowledgeable about their needs and milestones is crucial. While passion comes first, training enhances your ability to create an enriching and supportive environment for children.

While degrees are awesome and show you were consistent in your learning and follow-through, they are not necessary in this field. Personally, I only have fifteen ECE units. When hiring teachers over the years, I have always said that you either have the passion for this job, or you don't. I strongly encourage individuals entering this field to pursue basic early childhood education (ECE) courses. These courses can provide valuable knowledge and skills to support your journey. Additionally, safety training is of utmost importance.

As a preschool owner, you have the responsibility of safeguarding the well-being of the children in your care. CPR/first aid training is mandatory, as well as training on mandated reporting, sanitation, and bookkeeping. In California, for example, you must maintain a comprehensive file for each student, including emergency pickup forms, vaccination records, and allergy information. As you hire teachers, it becomes your responsibility to train and educate them. Each new employee should receive thorough training on your program, philosophy, daily schedule, and emergency protocols.

Children, as we know, get into everything, and they are extremely fast. Safety should always be at the forefront of your mind, whether that's always keeping an eye on your students or sweeping sand from the sidewalk to prevent a fall.

Training comes in lots of different ways, and continuing education is essential for personal and professional growth. Attend workshops, seminars, and conferences to expand your knowledge and stay updated on the latest research and trends in early childhood education. These events offer opportunities to connect with other professionals, exchange ideas, and learn from experienced speakers.

One area where training and technology intersect is software and technology for preschool management. Explore software solutions that can help you streamline bookkeeping, record-keeping, lead generation, and client tracking. Embracing technology can enhance your organization, efficiency, and communication with parents. I only recently implemented software for billing and credit cards. Why I waited on this, I am not sure. It's amazing, and we love it and the tracking of our students. When you are a small home-based business, I don't think it's necessary, but as you grow, I highly encourage you to get training on all the new and efficient technology software out there to help your business perform at a higher level.

Remember, training should be an ongoing process in all aspects of your business. Continuously seek opportunities to learn, grow, and improve. The more knowledge and skills you acquire, the better equipped you'll be to provide high-quality education and care for young children.

Training also includes spending a good amount of time with your team. Your team members are a direct reflection of you, and how you want them to represent your brand is vital. Training also includes team bonding. A team that gets along and are friends creates a family atmosphere and team longevity. I typically do a team-bonding social one month and a team staff meeting the next. The director of my school also does twice-a-month one-on-one meetings with staff to check in to see how they are or if they have any concerns or questions.

Training is always ongoing. This includes clear expectations and communication. Ongoing training will keep your program running smoothly and successfully for the long haul. While passion is the driving force behind your work in early childhood education, training plays a critical role in enhancing your skills and knowledge. Combine your passion with continuous learning and training to create a solid foundation for your preschool program and ensure its success for years to come.

Journal Prompt

In what areas do you think you need more training?

CHAPTER TWENTY-ONE

"U" is for Understanding

"Listening is not understanding the words of the question asked, listening is understanding why the question was asked in the first place."
—Simon Sinek

Understanding is a fundamental aspect of being an educator. It involves listening attentively, offering support, and comprehending the needs of those around you.

As educators, our top priority is understanding the needs of our students. By actively listening and paying attention to their cues, words, and needs, we can build trust and establish a loving relationship. Understanding the needs of different age groups allows us to instill in each child a lifelong love of learning and create a safe environment where they can truly flourish. Understanding all the different people who walk through your doors is key for long-term success, from your team members to your clients and students.

Everyone wants to be heard and understood, us included. The word *grace* remains at the forefront of my mind. Just as we need grace because none of us are perfect, and life is beautifully messy, so do our team and clients. Life can throw some curveballs, and you never know what people are truly going through.

Learning should be a joyful and lighthearted experience, filled with hands-on activities that foster growth at every step. Patience is essential in understanding your students, even on challenging days. In the field of early childhood education, one of the most beautiful aspects is how children can teach us something new every day, offering pure and unconditional love. It is a blessed and amazing gift to be allowed into their hearts and lives.

Understanding others extends beyond the students in your care. It also involves comprehending the needs and concerns of the parents and clients. Listening is a gift that can often be overlooked in the fast-paced world we live in. Instead of imposing our opinions or adopting a my-way-or-the-highway approach, it is crucial to approach interactions with grace and compassion. We are all human, with our own stories and challenges. Each person carries burdens that may not be visible on the surface.

Running a preschool involves navigating the complexities of human interaction. Some children may present difficult behaviors, and it is important to try to understand the "why" behind their actions and the background they come from. Many individuals are hurting and struggling, and empathy can make a significant difference in their lives. At times, parents may find solace in your office, sharing their stories and situations, and it is a privilege to provide them with support. In today's world, social media often presents a polished and idealized version of life, but in reality, life is beautifully messy. There are ups and downs, and understanding this duality is essential. The job of an early childhood educator is one of service, and the rewards far outweigh the challenges faced daily.

If you ever feel tempted to leave this field, remember that it is a calling deeply ingrained in your being. Embrace the messy beauty of life and the transformative impact you can have on children's lives.

I am not a trained therapist—far from it—but so many times in this role, I am gifted the opportunity to listen and give support. From a diagnosis of cancer and unexpected deaths in families to divorce and a vast array of emotional stress, I have had clients break down in my office. Being real, honest, and open to understanding creates valuable trust with your clients.

Even recently, I had a raw interaction with a parent as they were vulnerable and open about a difficult life challenge. I listened and listened some more, and afterward, I was reminded once again why I do what I do. It's a gift, and I don't take that lightly.

You can either judge and brush off difficult clients, or you can take the time to understand why they may be difficult.

Leadership in the field of early childhood education requires grace, compassion, and flexibility. It is about creating boundaries and expectations with love and empathy rather than micromanaging. Recognize that each member of your team brings their own expertise, ideas, and creativity to the classroom. Encourage them to shine individually and collectively, empowering them to see their potential and celebrating their unique contributions.

Ultimately, it is important to remember that behind the budgets, the business aspect, and the daily operations, we are all human beings trying to navigate life's journey. We are all figuring it out as we go, and understanding and supporting one another is the key to success.

Journal Prompt

What are some ways you can help foster understanding and compassion in your business?

CHAPTER TWENTY-TWO

"V" Is for Validation

"The only permission, the only validation, and the only opinion that matters in our quest for greatness in our own."
—Dr. Steve Maraboli

Becoming your own boss is an exciting and fulfilling endeavor akin to achieving one of life's greatest accomplishments. As a business owner, you have the freedom to set your own rules, create a unique vibe, and be at the helm of your enterprise. However, it's crucial to recognize the weight of this role and the responsibilities that come with it. Being a boss is not about exerting control or enforcing arbitrary rules, but rather about shouldering the immense responsibility of supporting numerous families and their livelihoods. It's about fulfilling the promises you made when hiring your team and delivering on those commitments with respect and accountability.

I honestly don't like being called "Boss." I look at myself as a team member, and when I am in my schools, I'm jumping in to help. Whether it's changing a diaper, emptying trash, or even cleaning the bathrooms, I think good leadership isn't being a micromanager but allowing your team members to shine. You've hired them to do just that—shine.

A good boss recognizes the value of a team. I love, love my team, and I try my hardest to show them how much they are appreciated, from monthly first-of-the-month gifts, staff socials, and Christmas parties to an end-of-the-year wine tasting and ample time off to rest and recuperate.

When you step into this next role as boss, there isn't anyone above you to shower you with praise or monthly gifts. You are the top, so your validation and praise come from within, and your freedom to make your own schedule to come and go is your praise. You just need to remind yourself you made it to the top.

Being the boss, you have the heavy burden of being responsible for other people and their families. I know when I give out paychecks, it's helping support a family, and that is a burden I don't take lightly. One vital aspect of being a responsible boss is ensuring that payroll is always on time. Paying your staff promptly demonstrates your appreciation for their hard work, love, and dedication to your business. They have poured their time, energy, and soul into your venture, and they deserve to feel valued and respected. Cherishing and safeguarding a good team is essential.

Yet, being a boss can sometimes feel lonely. As you ascend to the top, there's no one above you to cheer you on or provide validation. Your new role as an owner entails becoming the cheerleader for your team, supporting and encouraging each member individually. Celebrate your team's achievements and show your appreciation through gestures like showering them with gifts during staff appreciation week.

One of the most challenging lessons to learn as a boss is the separation of friendship and business. When running a small business, it's common to develop close relationships with your team. However, blurring the lines between being a boss and a friend can lead to complications. Finding a balance between being too close and maintaining a professional distance is crucial. Your primary focus should be validating and supporting your team rather than seeking validation for yourself. Validation as a business owner comes from your clients and students as they recognize the excellence of your program and spread positive word-of-mouth.

Expanding and growing your business often necessitates adopting a CEO mindset and separating business decisions from personal relationships. While your team may feel like family and friends due to their long-standing dedication, it's important to prioritize what is best for the entire business. Protect the collective rather than focusing solely on one individual. If a team member exhibits negative behavior, creates drama, or fosters a toxic atmosphere, address the issue promptly. Avoid waiting for change that may never come, as it can be detrimental to the team as a whole. Be a strong leader and act decisively when necessary.

I remember when that shift from boss to CEO happened. It was in 2010 when I opened my first center and then my second center in a span of six months. I went from three employees to twelve, and I really felt the shift. I had to make hard decisions, and I now had a bigger team and two schools to think about, not just my home-based little school. It was a big change, and it took me a while to shift into a role based more on decision-making and less on friendship. I had to constantly think of the bigger picture regarding the business, and I didn't just have three staff members to think about—I had twelve.

I learned that my team didn't see the behind-the-scenes of the financials. Your team members are there to come and do their job and then go home and not have to think about the business; that's the beautiful thing about being an employee. But as an employer, you don't get to shut your job off at 5:00 p.m. Being the boss is a twenty-four-hour job. Now, of course, you have boundaries and can set up office hours, but if something is broken at your school, you are fixing it no matter what time it is. You are responsible for every aspect of the entire business, and if something goes wrong, it falls on you and you alone.

As a boss, you may sometimes feel overwhelmed and uncertain of which direction to take. During such moments, it's important to prioritize self-care and find solace in stillness. Taking time for yourself, whether through travel, hiking, or simply staying at home, allows you to regroup and gather your thoughts. Internal validation is crucial for your role as the owner, CEO, or boss.

No matter how much effort you put in or how much you care for your staff, complaints and dissatisfaction will always arise. Understand that it is impossible to please everyone at all times, and accept that being perfect is an unattainable ideal. Over time, you will develop resilience and learn not to take hurtful comments personally. To cultivate empathy and understanding, try placing yourself in the shoes of others. While we only see our own perspectives and experiences, a good leader strives to comprehend different viewpoints. Just as you are seeking personal growth and new challenges by reading this book, understand that your team members also aspire for more in their lives. Recognizing this innate human desire for growth allows you to foster individual and collective development through validation and support.

Feeling lonely as a boss is natural at times, but remember to acknowledge and appreciate your accomplishments. Reflect on what you have built and the positive impact you have had on others. Networking with fellow business owners can provide a valuable support system, allowing you to connect with like-minded individuals who understand the unique challenges you face. Being your own boss has countless beautiful and rewarding aspects. It grants you the freedom to be an active parent while pursuing your passion as a businessperson. It offers financial stability and empowers you to stand on your own feet.

I am so grateful that I believed in myself all those years ago. Being my own boss has been one of my greatest adventures. My praise comes from the pride I have when I step back at school events and see just how many families we touch during the year. My business journey has allowed me to grow, break free from unhealthy situations, and achieve personal and professional independence. Embrace the validation that comes from within and be grateful for the seed of an idea that blossomed into a breathtaking reality. When you feel lonely, remember that you made it to the top, and remind yourself of what you created and the impact you are making.

Journal Prompt

Why do you want to be your own boss?

CHAPTER TWENTY-THREE

"W" is for Wage

*"Paying good wages is not charity at all—
it is the best kind of business."*
—Henry Ford

The topic of wages and payroll can be uncomfortable and overwhelming, especially for small business owners. As much as we want to pay our staff as much as possible, the reality is that your preschool is a business, and profitability is essential for long-term success. Managing wages requires a delicate balance and careful consideration of your budget. I must admit that it's an ongoing challenge for me as well when it comes to sending out teacher contracts and making job offers each year. Even when running your business from home, it's crucial to establish legitimacy and professionalism right from the start.

Paying employees in cash under the table is not only illegal but can also lead to significant consequences if discovered. Building a reputable image within your community and among your peers is important, so I highly recommend being legal and legitimate from the beginning.

Now, let's break down some business terminology. Please note that I am not an attorney or an expert in this field; I'm simply sharing my experiences as a business owner who has grown her business and adhered to legal requirements.

When I started my business from home, I operated as a sole proprietor. I recommend researching this term to understand its implications fully. Even as a non-expert, I opened a professional bank account under my business name and established an account with the Employment Development Department (EDD). Recognizing my strengths and weaknesses, I hired a bookkeeper and a payroll professional right away to ensure compliance and mitigate any risks. As I expanded my business and opened a second location, I followed the advice of my professional CPA and formed a corporation. Here are a few key steps to set up your small business for success:

- **Separate business bank account:** Creating a separate bank account for your business helps keep your personal and business finances separate for tax purposes and simplifies bookkeeping at the end of the year.

- **Payroll service:** If you plan on hiring employees, consider using a payroll service to handle payroll calculations and tax deductions and ensure compliance with labor laws.

- **Bookkeeper:** Hiring a bookkeeper can help you keep your financial records organized and ready for tax purposes. QuickBooks Online is a popular and reliable tool for this purpose.

- **EDD account:** Establish an account with the Employment Development Department to handle unemployment payments and taxes. Your payroll professional can assist you in setting this up correctly.

- **Liability insurance:** Prioritize obtaining liability insurance to protect your business, even if you have just a few students or a larger enrollment. This is a crucial step to safeguard your business from potential lawsuits and unexpected incidents.

- **Workers' compensation insurance:** If you have employees, it's essential to have workers' compensation insurance to cover work-related injuries or illnesses. This insurance is typically mandatory for all employees.

Remember, it's crucial to consult with professionals, such as attorneys, CPAs, and insurance agents, who can provide expert guidance tailored to your specific circumstances. Their expertise will ensure that you comply with legal and financial requirements, allowing you to focus on providing a quality preschool experience for your students and maintaining a sustainable business.

Managing payroll and ensuring fair compensation for your staff is an ongoing process that requires careful consideration of your budget and legal obligations. By prioritizing professionalism and seeking appropriate support, you can navigate this aspect of business ownership successfully. Compensation plays a crucial role in attracting and retaining a dedicated and passionate team.

While some may question your approach based on standard payroll percentages, it's important to remember that every business is unique, and it's ultimately up to you to determine how you want to allocate your budget. The preschool business has its limitations when it comes to pricing and capacity. Tuition fees and the number of students you can enroll directly impact the funds available for wages. Being mindful of this, I recommend you make the choice to invest in your team by offering competitive compensation.

By paying your staff well, you attract high-quality candidates and foster stability and loyalty within your team. This leads to a positive impact on the overall quality of education and care provided to the children.

Other schools may inadvertently reveal their wage structure through the caliber of their staff, which is a testament to the connection between compensation and the quality of educators, highlighting the importance of building a stable and outstanding team to create demand for your school. A high turnover rate can be disruptive and hinder the progress of your preschool, while a committed and talented team elevates your institution's reputation. Therefore, you should be willing to take a slight hit financially to ensure the stability and excellence of your crew.

While you may not offer health benefits at this time, you may choose to provide other perks, like a 401(k) and ample vacation time. Paid time off should be generous, and I like to align it with the local school district's calendar. This consistency allows your team to plan and enjoy time off alongside their families and get the well-deserved rest they need. Set your payroll budget based on the number of students enrolled each fall. This shows your commitment to rewarding your staff's dedication and loyalty. Additionally, organizing staff socials and offering monthly gifts are thoughtful gestures that demonstrate your appreciation for their hard work and contribution.

A great team is the key to success in this business. Their dedication and passion can take your preschool to new heights. By fostering a supportive and rewarding environment, you are building a strong foundation for your business to thrive.

Remember to continue adapting and evolving as your business grows. Seek feedback from your team and remain open to their needs and aspirations. By nurturing and investing in your staff, you are creating an environment where everyone can flourish, resulting in a positive impact on the children and families you serve.

As the cost of living increases over time due to inflation, it's essential to provide annual wage increases to your long-term staff members. Offering regular raises helps maintain their financial well-being and acknowledges their dedication and commitment to your preschool. Consistent wage increases demonstrate that you value your employees and recognize their contribution to the success of your business. They also help create a sense of security and job satisfaction, which can contribute to your team's long-term retention and overall morale.

When considering annual wage increases, it's important to assess your budget and revenue growth to ensure you can sustainably accommodate these adjustments. Consider factors such as inflation rates, local industry standards, and the financial performance of your preschool. Additionally, it's beneficial to have a structured performance evaluation system in place. Regular performance assessments provide an opportunity to assess individual staff members' progress, identify areas for improvement, and reward outstanding performance through merit-based raises. Open communication with your team about wage adjustments is crucial. Transparently explain the rationale behind the increases and how they align with the growth and success of your preschool. Encourage feedback and address any questions or concerns they may have. Remember that fair and competitive wages not only help retain your experienced staff but also attract new talent.

Offering a compensation package that is competitive within the industry can be a significant factor for potential employees when considering joining your team. Continuously monitor wage trends and market conditions in your area to ensure your compensation remains competitive. This ongoing evaluation will allow you to make informed decisions about wage adjustments and demonstrate your commitment to supporting your staff's financial well-being. It took me a little while to realize that my team is going to talk, and they love to tell each other how much they make. So, creating a solid, clear payroll scale is ideal. The way I do it is everyone gets paid the same based on how many years they have worked and their education. So if they do share, there are no surprises, and they each make the same in the year category they are in.

MS. AMBER JAYNE

Journal Prompt

How much do other preschools in your area pay their teachers?

CHAPTER TWENTY-FOUR

"X" is for X Marks the Spot

*"X marks the spot for where are you right now.
Live into every moment with purpose and passion."*
—Kira Bruno

Setting up a classroom is indeed an exciting process, and it's wonderful to feel enthusiasm for creating a welcoming and homey environment for your students. This part is one of my favorites. Creating a fun, warm, and inviting classroom is thrilling. I love going to Pinterest for ideas, and I've always strived for a homey feel. Remember—this is your students' home away from home, Monday–Friday. I know many schools scream preschool, with primary colors and lots of paper bulletin board items all around. I started like that years ago, but over the years, I've gone more to a shabby Pottery Barn–style look.

Once you figure out what look you want, you will then need to create your classroom areas for learning. Here are the main areas of my classroom must-haves:

Circle Time Area:
- Calendar to review days of the week, months, and important dates.
- Job chart to assign and rotate classroom responsibilities.
- Numbers and letters, focusing on one each week.

- Visual aids or props related to monthly themes or topics.
- Class mascot for students to take turns bringing home with a journal.
- Whiteboard or easel for letter and number reviews.
- Use a music machine or Amazon Alexa for music and movement activities.
- Instruments and ribbons for interactive music sessions.
- Cozy rug to define the space and make it inviting.

Art Area/Learning Centers:
- Table and chairs for art activities and small-group work.
- Shelves to organize art supplies like paper, paints, markers, and pencils.
- An art drying rack is used to display and store artwork.
- Bulletin boards to showcase students' art projects.
- Scissors and glue for arts-and-crafts projects.
- Sink nearby for easy cleanup.

This area can also serve as a versatile space for other activities, such as eating, learning centers, dittos, science projects, and hands-on learning

Block Area:
- A variety of building blocks for imaginative play and creativity.
- Toys like trains, cars, dinosaurs, and animals to enhance play scenarios.
- Enough space for children to spread out and explore their ideas.

Dramatic Play Area:
- A role-playing space that fosters real-life scenarios and encourages social interactions, problem-solving, and creativity.
- Items like a play kitchen, baby dolls, household items, and props.

Quiet Area:
- A cozy corner with a rug, pillows, and soft lighting.
- Books, both fiction and non-fiction, for children to read independently.
- Calm and relaxing atmosphere where students can take breaks when needed.

Playground
- An engaging outdoor exploration area.
- Climbing structures, balls, bikes, sandbox, and water table.
- Designated garden areas with edible veggies.

Remember to personalize the classroom setup based on your preferences and the age group you're working with. Since I love a shabby chic or Pottery Barn style, consider using soft colors, comfortable seating, and decorative elements that create a warm and inviting atmosphere. Make sure your classroom is organized and clutter-free, with ample storage for materials and resources. I love using baskets for toy storage, creating a natural look. This is where you can be creative and bring your passions to life in your space. Remember, first impressions are huge, and a clean classroom that looks and smells welcoming is always a warm welcome to parents.

Enjoy the process of designing your classroom, and may it become a nurturing and inspiring space for your students to learn and grow!

CHAPTER TWENTY-FIVE

"Y" is for You've Got This

"When you have a dream, you've got to grab it and never let go."
—Carol Burnett

You made it this far! Congratulations! You may be well on your way to opening your own preschool.

I know I covered a lot in this book, but I want to say, "You've got this!"

If you love early learners and are passionate about making a difference in children's lives and your community, this can be one of the best adventures of your life. It's not an easy job by any means, but the rewards and joy this career can bring are overwhelming at times.

Little ones need good, strong, and kind leaders to help them be the best versions of themselves. We desperately need more early educators to provide quality, loving programs.

Your investment can be sustained and grow because young children always need preschool and care. The early education industry is an $18 billion business.

For me, running Loving Start since 2001 has brought me great joy. There have been some tears along the way as well, but mostly so much joy. I never grew up thinking I would be doing this: running schools being a boss babe, but I think it was exactly what I was supposed to do. I've tried a few times to do something else, but I have always come back to early learners.

I truly believe if you have the passion, you, too, can become a successful boss and run a prosperous, quality preschool program. When I was younger, I just wanted to provide for my family; I wanted to feel like I was contributing to our family budget. That's where this little seed of an idea started. All of our dreams start with an idea, and whether you choose to nurture that seed determines if it will blossom into something beautiful. Are you ready to water your seed? Are you ready to put in the hard work and maybe some tears along the way to see your dream come true? You've got this if you want it.

I know you, too, can create financial stability, all while making an impact on your clients. I encourage you to continue to journal, write down your ideas, and do your homework. Research your competition, take the ECE classes, and create and design your dream school. I never saw myself still doing this after twenty-five years, but looking ahead, I can see another twenty-five, just maybe in a different capacity.

I have loved being my own boss. As a mother, it truly gave me the opportunity to be there for my kids. I really believe I had the best of both worlds; I was an active mom and businesswoman. I don't think I could ever go back to working for someone else. The freedom this career has given me is priceless.

I truly hope this guidebook has helped you get excited about the possibility and reality of becoming your own boss! You've got this! As you begin to create your dream school, also remember to create it with boundaries in mind and implement time for yourself to recharge.

Journal Prompt

Thoughts on everything you've learned:

CHAPTER TWENTY-SIX
"Z" is for Zoom Away

"Zoom in, zoom out, but never lose your focus."
—Shikha TD

It's time to officially wrap this up. My wish for you is that you will take the knowledge I've learned over the past twenty-five years and zoom away to creating your own dream preschool. Take your journal notes and begin to research the schools in your area to see how you can shine independently from them. If you haven't yet taken early childhood education classes, sign up for them today. Immerse yourself in early childhood education to see where your passions will fall within your philosophy. I hope by sharing my failures and my successes, I can help you be well on your way—faster and more efficiently.

My wish is that you have the life you've always imagined for yourself. Our journey here is short in the grand scheme of things. Our job is such a huge part of our life and very essence. I know for me, personally, I only want to do what brings me joy. I just don't have the time or energy to waste on things that don't bring me joy. Life is precious, and waking up happy doing work that is impactful and of service brings me great joy. What do you desire? Where do you see yourself in a year? Is this the career for you? Do you feel it deep in your soul that this may be your path? You'll feel it, believe me. If you can feel it stirring, if you feel the butterflies and the ideas flowing, you're on the right path. You've got this; you really do! I believe in you!

Thank you so much for giving me the opportunity to share my passion for little ones with you and for teaching the next generation of early educators. We need more educators who prioritize love and kindness to wrap up our next generation of children with love and excitement for learning. Don't give up when things get hard. This new journey will be difficult to start and navigate at first, but don't be discouraged; the reward will outweigh the hard, trust me. Just keep persevering—zooming forward, my friend.

I'll leave you with my favorite quote I've used for almost my entire time running Loving Start: "Wish It, Dream It, Do It."

Cheers to love and new beginnings as a preschool owner and making a huge positive impact on all you serve!

THANK YOU FOR READING MY BOOK!

Thank you for buying and reading my book. I would love to give you a couple of free resources!

Scan the QR Code Here:

I appreciate your interest in my book and value your feedback as it helps me improve future versions of this book. I would appreciate it if you could leave your invaluable review on Amazon.com with your feedback. Thank you!

www.ingramcontent.com/pod-product-compliance
Lightning Source LLC
Chambersburg PA
CBHW032122090426
42743CB00007B/432